BANISHING THE BOOGIEMAN

Politics is personal

Banishing the Boogieman

Jill Parris

Copyright © Jill Parris 2015

First published January 2015

ISBN 978-1-942574-80-4

BANISHING THE BOOGIEMAN

'No longer able to change a situation - we are challenged to change ourselves.'

Victor E. Frankl

DEDICATION

This book is dedicated to Mike and Des

Your home has always been my refuge

FOREWORD

I have wondered should I persevere with my story? Now I am sure. People need to know the consequences of living in the shadows of an unjust regime.

On the 10th December, 2014 I listened to a speech given by former Prime Minister Malcolm Fraser at the opening of new premises for the Asylum Seeker Resource Centre (ASRC) in Footscray choked with tears.

Mr. Fraser thanked the ASRC 'As so often happens in Australia, when there is a real need, people come forth to help with generosity and compassion' but he continued 'Australia's name has been damaged around the world. We are known as the most inhumane, the most uncaring, the most selfish of all the wealthy countries. It used not to be that way. This is the journey we have travelled since Tampa.'[1]

'Our democratic system depends on the "rule of law"; it depends on due process, on properly produced evidence, on precedents and on a process that is open to appeal by a higher authority.' This legislation[2] gives to the minister . . . total arbitrary, dictatorial powers over the lives and fortunes of asylum seekers. It destroys the "rule of law" as we know it.'

'Under the UN Refugee Convention, which Menzies signed onto in 1954, boat people were not illegal. The treaty says that those fleeing terror often travel by

---

[1] In August 2001, the Howard Government of Australia refused permission for the Norwegian freighter MV Tampa, carrying 438 rescued refugees to enter Australian waters.

[2] Migration and Maritime Powers Legislation Amendment (the Asylum Legacy Caseload) Bill 2014 Migration and Maritime Powers Legislation Amendment (the Asylum Legacy Caseload) Bill 2014

unorthodox means and often without papers . . . The minister's decisions are (now) absolute. The determination procedures have been short-circuited to such an extent that any legitimate examination of a boat person's case would be almost impossible. This is a far cry from the Australia we used to know, but it is today's Australia.

'This new law strips out references to the UN Refugee Convention' and is 'replaced by a new definition of refugee' so that 'Australia can now return an asylum seeker to a country where they may be tortured. The new law removes any existing checks and balances that provide protections for those seeking asylum.

'The minister's powers are outside the "rule of law", beyond appeal. He has the powers of a tyrant. We should not pretend that this is just a minor change. It presents a destruction of democratic process.

'We might spare a thought for the future. Today the bill applies to asylum seekers but it establishes a new practice beyond the "rule of law". If there is another group that this government does not like will it extend that practice to them?'

Thank you Mr. Fraser for welcoming me to Australia in 1980 when I fled oppression and now for standing against the erosion of democracy.

OUR FAMILY

The mountains

When the moon above the ridges, silvers all the fields below
And the gentle mountain breezes softly come and softly go
When the streams of winding water sing an evening melody
In the Transvaal hills and valleys, there you'll find the heart of me.

I have seen the Alpine splendour, forests green and pearly snow
Wandered in the lovely lake land where the daffodils do grow
Lovely beauty lies among them but wherever I may be
In the Transvaal hills and valleys you will find the heart of me.
~

If I squeeze my eyes closed tight, I can remember a time when Mummy, Daddy, Peter and I were really happy. That was before the Boogieman.

The time was 1953; the place Johannesburg in South Africa. On weekends, we would go to the mountains. Mummy and Daddy would pack the tent, the sleeping bags, food, torches, a lead for our Scottie, Russell, and oranges to eat on our way up the mountain. I loved camping even though it was a very big walk.

We'd get in the car and I'd sit on a big cushion to see out the window, Peter would sit in his booster seat, and Russell would sit between us and play a game putting his wet nose against our legs. It would tickle, he'd bark and we'd giggle. Sometimes Mummy and Daddy would sing in German and sometimes they'd sing about the 'hills and valleys' and Peter and I would join in and then Peter would laugh and laugh.

When we got to Mr. Coetzee's farm, we'd park in a line, say hello to other climbers, put on our packs and say thanks to Mr. Coetzee. He'd take our 'two and six', push his dentures out and we'd laugh and say goodbye and begin our trek up the mountain.

It was hard to walk because I was little and had a big pack with my own sleeping bag. The grass would tickle my nose and I could hardly see over but the sun would shine and I'd walk with Russell who'd run off and come back wagging his tail. Peter would point and chat from his sitting place on top of Daddy's pack.

1

There was a path up the hill, the grass was golden, and big fluffy seeds blew in the breeze. Mummy and her friends would stop, chat, wait for us kids, and give us a gulp of water before we went on. Always hot, we walked slowly, stopping often to sigh and say how tired we were. I would beg ' carry me', but Daddy would say,

'Come now Ponkie, you're big. Russell is with you and your friends. It's not much longer to the top.'

When we got to the saddle at the top of the ridge, Dad would stop, peel an orange with his special pocketknife and cut the skin from the top to the bottom in little orange leaves carefully burying the peel 'because it takes ages to rot.' Then he'd sit and divide the orange into four. Peter got the smallest because he was little and got a ride. Then he'd stretch out his hand to me 'Here you are Ponkie, eat carefully and don't dribble because there's nowhere to wash until we get to camp.'

'Daddy, Peter messed his orange and threw it on the ground and only had the juice.'

'That's fine, Ponkie, the pith will rot soon or the ants will come. Now off you go with Russell and the others. I'll follow soon with Peter.'

Once over the saddle, I could stand on a big rock, look down across the vast khaki grassland scattered about with huge boulders and thorn trees and down to a big gorge cut through the mountains. Still quite a way for little legs but downhill and I knew the path to the natural rock fortress where we camped. With Russell at my side I was quite happy to lead the way, quite proud. Leading was important to learn properly to become a real mountaineer and not just a tripper. Daddy's rules for responsible mountaineers were plentiful. 'Respect the land. Leave the mountain exactly as it was before you got there. No rubbish, no litter, no equipment so that when others come they will do likewise. Never leave food out for monkeys because they must survive on the land. Never leave fires going even in the special fireplaces we have built and make sure others do likewise. When you climb always have a companion and don't tackle any climb beyond your capability.'

Not always sure what Daddy was saying I knew what he said was important so I listened and tried to learn. My Daddy was good at everything in the mountains and people did what he said.

Once we reached our campsite, Daddy would make a fire and Mummy and Daddy would have their cup of Rooibos tea. We would drink crystal clear water Mummy had fetched from the stream with the tadpoles and daddy long legs. Then we'd set up camp. I would hold the tent pole as Daddy put big rocks on the pegs to hold it straight and stiff so no rain would come in. Then Peter would play building rock towers in the campsite while Daddy, Mummy and I joined the other campers looking for firewood for cooking and the campfire.

When at last all work was done we'd go for a swim or, if it was late, join other campers for sundowners before cooking and bed. 'Well how was court this week Tom?'

'The usual - stolen goods, fighting. Armed robbery up a bit.'

Doctor long-legs Bob would say, 'A couple of bad knife fights at the hospital. No black on white reports but trouble in Soweto.'

Uncle Dennis would ask 'How's business, Hans' and daddy would say, 'Good week and Else sold well. She was written up in the local rag.' The grownups would chatter and cook and we'd run around or sit and listen. The great big blue sky would go yellow and pink and then Venus would come out and Daddy would say, 'Can you see the Southern Cross yet?'

Next morning we'd leap out of our sleeping bags as the sun rose and make breakfast; the climbers would decide who was climbing and whose turn it was to take us kids to the rock pools. Then we'd snake down to the stream.

I can still see the beautiful big pool shining glassy and clear at the confluence of two streams. Here the water ripples and swirls before crashing forty meters to the cliff floor. Further down this larger stream the climbers would spend their day with ropes and pitons, scaling the cool vertical cliffs of the tree-filled valley. Above this pool the valley opened onto a great rocky ledge next to a small shallow stream. Here our minders chatted as we kids scrambled on the rocks around them. 'Be careful Jill, some rocks are sharp and watch your brother!'

I can feel the warmth of the summer sun, hear our giggles and the gurgling water between my toes. I was happy. My family's best days were spent in the mountains beside or in the water and at night well fed and protected from the cool night air by sleeping bags and a crackling fire we snuggled together. Above the sky sprinkled with stars; below a chorus of voices in several languages. The adults, now well oiled, sang, thrashed out political differences and shared hopes for the futures of their country and themselves. Uncle Denis would tease Daddy, 'Well you raving racist, how have you undermined our Government this week?'

'Oh! Letter dropping, explaining that your Nationalist brethren are getting more and more like the Nazis. Soon it'll be OK to kill a black man because he walks city streets.'

'Soon? We have to show them we're in charge. You bloody foreigners think you know best. Go back home. Oh sorry! I forgot they don't like jumped up Jewish trouble makers in Germany either.' Then he'd laugh and smack Daddy on the shoulders and say. 'Just kidding. You are welcome here.'

Around the fire, everyone was 'white'. But within these strict South African constraints, there was no creed or class - just compatriots sharing their love of camping, climbing, intellectual argument and strong appetites for living life fully. The hidden agendas were not part of my awareness. I smiled, sang and fought sleep. When I finally succumbed, I never woke until morning and my dreams were sweet.

This was before the Boogieman.

TRAUMA

Ruptures

Cape Town was stunning, but Johannesburg was the city of gold. So when I was just over two, our family packed up and moved so Dad could seek his fortune. Mum cursed. She was comfortable in the small flat in a bohemian suburb of a city at the southernmost point of Africa and didn't want to move. She'd miss living among her Kameraden youth group compatriots. They had fled together from Germany.

Mum never liked Jo'burg and her only respite came in the mountains surrounded by people sharing her interests. In the city we lived a car ride away from any friends and Mum was resentful that Dad didn't buy a larger house in a more affluent suburbs. She never let Dad forget this. I cannot remember a time of peace.

Tension was always palpable in our family.

An icy cold calm foreshadowed every storm. Slow rumbles of thunderous anger would swell, fill the air, hover and reverberate, as Peter and I backed away from our parents and hid in our bedroom or the kitchen and waited. Voices would rise to a crescendo, a plate, chair or table would smash against a wall or thud into a body, and misery would spread throughout the house. Then, just as suddenly the fury would dissipate into silent screams, eerie calm and the fragile darkness of the night.

In Johannesburg Dad bought a small cottage on a large corner block of land, our house an island separated from others by two roads, a vacant lot on one side and a drainage easement on another. Here in a solid, almost middle class, English-speaking neighborhood my parents recreated a small replica of the distinctive modern Bauhaus culture brought from their native Germany. Every rustic corner carefully crafted to capture the essence of simple sophistication.

But the vicious fights were also part of the furniture. Mum would sit cross-legged on a couch, back straight, wiry black hair standing out from her angular face, her piercing blue eyes animated as she listened to the sweet sounds of Mozart. She would run her fingers over the sensual thickness of the

5

sumptuous wine red mohair covering scattered with many colorful cushions, and smile as she relished the rich contrasts of the handsome, vegetable dyed, closely hand knotted Persian rug of geometric design against polished wooden boards.

She would rise and straighten the set of Bauhaus side tables, sit bolt upright once again and stare into the fire in its charming old hearth built of raw burgundy stock brick. Her gaze would move to the diamond pained leaded glass windows and down along the wooden bookshelves below. Her eyes would drink in a display of the *avant garde* with Sartre, Camus, Kierkegaard, Dostoyevsky, Nietzsche and Snow amongst other sources of angst and despair. This ritual followed by her looking up at the walls filled with an ever-changing array of pictures, in oils and pastels. Mum and two friends swapped these every six months for variety without too large an expense. The ambiance was the perfect embodiment of the expressionist era she has worked so hard at recreating in this place so far from the land of her birth.

Finally, she'd turn her gaze to a corner behind the fireplace where a black antique liquor cabinet with leaded glass doors stood below more shelves filled with art books that reached to the ceiling. She'd sigh, begin to fret, stand, straighten a picture and sit again.

Then Mum would stop looking, get up, open the liquor cabinet, pour herself a drink, return to the couch, pick up the newspaper and read. I'd flinch. Mum's drinking was addictive and her reading the paper with warnings of our troubled land a trigger I knew well.

Peter and I would sit on the carpet at Mum's feet. Not allowed to bring toys into the lounge we'd fidget as I teased Peter and Mum read. As minutes ticked by she'd begin to mutter 'If your father doesn't return soon the servants will be kept back again!' Fetching another drink, she'd become increasingly morose. Peter and I'd sit as quietly as we could and wait. By 6:00, she was primed to explode and by the time Dad came in just before six thirty, Mum would have her third drink in hand.

'Late again! What this time?' she'd snipe.

'Well hello Else dear. How was your day?' Had a little drink have you?'

6

'The servants have been on from six this morning and they only have Thursday afternoons and Saturdays off. They need some time to themselves and can't leave until the washing up is done and the table set for breakfast. I know they live on the property but how'd you like only ten hours a day to sleep and socialize you selfish sod? We need to eat.'

'I'll just wash up.'

'You bastard! Kids, into the dining room now.'

By the time Dad sat, it was hard to swallow.

Helpless, I'd stare past Dad at Peter. Meal times were important in our house because, 'Your father foraged for potato peelings to feed his family during the inflation'. But nothing would stop them now. Peter and I would sit frozen and silent, listen and wait while the storm grew, climaxed, something was broken or someone hurt. To move would attract attention and draw us into this unrelenting but predictable vortex.

On one occasion, hoping to draw Dad's attention away, I picked up the jug and moved my arm backwards to pitch milk at him but gravity took over. The jug fell and milk spilled everywhere. I was drenched. Mum slapped me across my milk white face and I ran out crying. Louisa, our maid, was in the kitchen. She wrapped me in her arms and I sobbed silently. Now the only sound from the dining room was the clink of cutlery against plates. Then the bell rang and Mum asked for the next course. Louisa gave me some dinner kept aside and I crept into bed.

Later I heard strange sounds from the other side of the wall. Sympathetic, loving whispers rose, became impassioned, changed to anger then full-blown fury. I held my breath and covered my head with a pillow. A crash and an uncanny scream dissipated into an unnatural quivering silence. The bedroom then the kitchen doors slammed and footsteps retreated into the night.

Next morning my parents weren't talking and Mum had a black eye. A chair had disappeared from my parent's bedroom but nothing had moved in the beautiful cozy lounge. All was in its place.

Perhaps Mum's shame about the bruise she covered with makeup led to my five-year-old conclusions that she was to blame. She had been drinking and had started the fight. Louisa was powerless as a black nanny, no one would listen to her. My attempt at distraction with milk had me hit, my last attempt to interfere when my parents fought. My first, but not my last, lesson in the powerless of children to stop adult violence.

***

Louisa did help me devising an escape plan. 'When you're scared, hide in my room under my bed. It is high up and is covered with a white sheet hanging to the floor. There's space for a girl and a bunny but be careful. My people have the Tokoloshe, a naughty little spirit and if he doesn't like you, he will make you sick. That is why my bed is on bricks. He is too small to reach me from the floor. He comes when it's dark and people sleep so I think you're safe and at night you can knock and I will let you in and close the door.'

There were times when I ran found Louisa's key, unlock her door and creep under her bed. Here I sat dead still and held my breath not sure, who was scarier Mum or the Tokoloshe. This grew, morphed, fueled my imagination and became my fear of Annihilation, the Boogieman who haunted my dreams.

***

Sometimes Mum's anger came directly at me, 'Look after Peter.' Slap.

'But . . .'

'Well out with it. Why not?'

'Sorry Mummy, he wanted . . . ' I duck out of her way.

'Get back here.' Peter comes into the kitchen stares open mouthed before scurrying away before Mum sees him.

'But' . . . and the burning sensation, of her open hand against my face again. This time her fingernail catches my eye. I scream run into the kitchen and hide on the kitchen chair next to the climbing cupboard and cry. I wonder what I've done wrong and resolve to do better. I'll look after Peter better act more adult and be very, very good so Daddy will come home early and they won't fight and we can all be happy.

Later Mum comes into the kitchen in tears,

'I'm sorry. Your eyelid is bleeding let me clean it.'

Despite my resolutions, I'm furious and let it show.

'No. Don't touch me!'

'I'm so sorry.'

'Leave me alone!' I turn away, confused by my mixed feelings. She hurts then says sorry. Why can't she stop hurting me in the first place? 'She can't do what she likes just because she's bigger then me. And Peter never says anything. He talks all the time so why not when Mummy blames me? It's not fair! But I need to be good so they will stop . . .'

I saw the evidence of Daddy hitting Mummy, I never saw him do it. Nor see him throw anything. He never hit me either, so he was the safe parent, and I couldn't risk losing what little security he provided.

When totally bereft, I would turn to a self-portrait in blue and charcoal pastels. It distilled the agony and alienation Hanns Katz felt as he waited for death, a knowing, depressed soul ready for his unbidden fate. Starring into his charcoal eyes I felt held, considered and calmed. Hanns knew my secrets and didn't tell. He sat quietly by when I could no longer hide my tears. He was constant and present.

Peter

However alone my parents' fighting made me feel, Peter my younger brother was with me. I see Peter standing in his cot. Less than two years old. I was five. He picks up his bottle and hurls it at the floor. I scream as it shatters into a million shards and before anyone reaches him Peter is among the splinters and the milk has rose red rivulets and I am filled with horror at my inability to save Peter from himself.

Peter was always a strange little man. As he took his first unsure steps, he walked upright, tummy slightly out, curly blond hair awry. His hands flapped as he talked. With head cocked to one side he listened and analyzed what people said. Always thinking, always interpreting, always telling. When he spoke, grown-ups listened. He didn't babble, or chatter as normal toddlers do. He was serious, grown up and superior. He had real conversations about adult things while I, a full three years older, was still dragged Bunny around by his ears.

As Peter took up more space in our family, I retreated out of sight to watch on, rather than get involved. I wanted to participate, but couldn't compete. Rex, my guardian, who had held me high and laughed with delight at my solemn tales about toes, teddies and toys, stopped listening to me when Peter came along. My brother, the wise one now, held his attention as Rex considered everything Peter said and responded by respectfully questioning each idea. Peter also got the best of Mummy and Daddy and every other grown-up. He was a wise, engaging, clever, eccentric little Jew.

Such precocity meant Peter found children boring and so avoided their company. Mum disapproved. From the age of five or six my job was to get him to play with other kids. 'Peter needs to play with children his own age, Take him out and get other children to talk to him.'

How could I do this? Peter had no interest in the other children, didn't even speak their language. His big words and concepts were beyond their interest. They built castles in sandpits while he discussed jet-propelled engines taking humans to the moon. I also found children difficult, but for different reasons. I stuttered and they laughed and teased. 'St-st-stupid slobby pig' and, as I got older, 'wee-wee girl' when family stress led to occasional toileting mishaps. Forced outside to 'play', I would hold Peter's hand until Mum closed the door. Then drop it. But this solved no problem. Aiming crowd's edge, Peter would follow. I'd keep my mouth closed and hope he'd do the same. Fat chance. He would jabber away unaware of the social jeopardy, while I died inside.

It was the same when Peter and I were alone together. Under the hose or at an early dinner in our room he'd talk and I'd nod so that he might think I could follow. I understood little of his grand ideas about the world. Mostly I remember us alone, while Mum worked, gardened, or us sitting together in the lounge, without toys to avoid Mum's wrath. She hated our untidiness. Peter listened to music, his whole being resonating with the complexity of an orchestra or picking out and singing a simple theme at the centre of an opus. I'd watch on in awe, feeling inadequate.

And so it went. Odd little Peter making grown-ups smile kindly but littlies laugh cruelly, while I looked at the ground and pushed him away, feeling guilty. As if it were my fault.

Only two instances found us on the same side of the fence, connected in the way I longed to be with another human being, even a brother like Peter. The first when we sang together with Dad and Mum. Mum would begin a German folk song in her beautiful clear contralto voice and Dad's resonant baritone would take up a deep variation on the tune. Peter and I would join in with our crystal clear sopranos in gentle synchrony to the melody. I would relish the generous harmony we so easily created together.

Our parent's violence also bonded us. When Dad and Mum shouted and threw things or slammed and hit and hurt we either sat dead still or huddled together as one. We would hide under the table or he in his bed and me in mine and wait for the battle to end. We never spoke, but I always felt we shared the terror and breath-baited anticipation of the explosion's end.

In truth, I was ambivalent about my brother. I loved Peter's capacity to devour knowledge and explore everything, the excitement created by his taking nothing at face value. But I feared his unpredictability; the way he forsook me when involved in his own creations. His endless striving to create and shape his own world foreshadowed his complete escape first into fantasy and then into the psychosis and mental illness that ravaged all our lives.

***

At the heart of my problems, and perhaps Peter's, were the betrayals and trauma that my parents brought to their marriage. They couldn't love each other or us because they were continual caught with seeking the illusive 'peace' denied them in their youth.

One night we ate early without Dad. Mum sat in the dining room with a gin and tonic, something she didn't do when Dad was there. I ask where's Daddy?'

'Away.'

'Where you came from?'

'Yes'

'With Hitler?'

'For God's sake, you know Hitler is dead.'

'But you said there's a new Hitler in South Africa and Daddy made you come to Africa and you want to be in Europe.'

Peter adds, 'Where Einstein and existential art come from . . . '

'Yes Peter, he knew I wanted to go to Europe but he had other things on his mind.'

'Mummy, are all Jewish people dead?'

'Eat and get out. Go to your room. I always have to deal with your incessant stupid questions? Your father probably took some other bloody woman with him and not me.'

Peter is dumbstruck. Mum doesn't utter another word; I turn to my plate in silence and choke down my dinner.

When Dad returns I ask, 'Where were you? Were you were with another woman?'

'What on earth are you on about?'

'Peter airplane has special guns to protect us against Hitler and a beautiful room with pictures and books . . . ' Peter now four speaks as Dad drops his bag, lifts him in his arms, nuzzles into his neck and kisses him on both cheeks. Peter giggles and puts his arms around Daddy's neck. Daddy stretches his arms out looks straight into Peter's eyes and says, 'Hello Son' and puts him down turns to me and says, 'I need to unpack. Where's your mother? Else . . . ' He ruffles my hair looks around and goes through to the kitchen. He comes back munching an apple, picks up his bag and heads for his bedroom, 'Else . . .'

'I'm busy.'

Daddy enters the bedroom talking loudly in German. Mum comes into the lounge pulls me up by the ear and clips me, 'This is for interfering!' She goes to the liqueur cabinet and pours a drink. I run out crying and Peter follows. We climb under the covers together; Peter turns on a torch and invites me to join him in his airplane. 'Nothing can hurt us here.' The shouting recedes.

'When my airplane comes true' . . . . . Peter draws word pictures of us escaping. We fly to Europe, America and Mars, protected by mighty defenses. His guns, missiles, radar detectors and smoke screens hide us and keep us safe.

Peter's airplane fantasy is consuming. He draws maps and writes lists in his own secret writing. Nothing is forgotten and no one else can read what he writes. He has lists of favorite foods, juices, toys for me, and books, puzzles and tools for him.

We hug; I stroke his hair and my little brother talks about what he can see and what he will do. The stories fade into sleep as we cling together. Warm and snug we shut the yelling out. He loves me, my big, brave, baby brother.

Next morning we wake, rub sleep from our eyes and remember our antipathy. There is a science book for Peter and a red hunters hat for me both gifts from Dad. I love the hat but give it to Peter. He says he will keep it safe for me in his airplane. I never see it again.

From that day on Peter's airplane becomes consuming and he goes there often. He mumbles to himself making plans to fix, build, hide, and fly. He sometimes talks about what he's done but never again asks me to join him. I wish I understood why but I don't. Only that he is gone and I am alone

And as Peter shuts himself away, Mum and Dad pursue him leaving me to watch. Dad asks him to talk about his wonderful airplane. Mum asks where he goes but I can see in their faces that they, like me, don't understand. All we know is his mind has gone to somewhere we can't follow. Only I know it was their fighting that saw Peter fly out of our reach.

Sad, I miss Peter. I'm cold, alone and when you are gone and Mummy and Daddy fight I begin having bad dreams where noises from the other side of the wall flourish and I am overshadowed by a big scary menace and begin to run from the Boogieman.

***

There were special times when Peter and I just had fun, usually when Mum and Dad were out.

Louisa and Tom, our household servants, ate different food, served in metal bowls at times outside their designated working hours. They shared food with each other from the same plate and ate with their fingers. Their main meal was mid-morning and sometimes if we were 'very good', Louisa would let us share with them. Sharing somehow made their food taste especially good.

This meal was often eaten outside in a spot warmed by the morning sun. Here Louisa and Tom and occasionally the nanny across the street would sit chat and take in the morning air as they ate.

For an hour, household duties stopped. Louisa and Tom relaxed and related to us as different people. Tom, a strapping black man with smiling brown eyes and peppercorn hair, a tribal worrier from generations of fighting men, spoke of his rich Zulu heritage in a quiet, gravelly voice filled with laughter. His people had protected Zululand against many marauding tribes including the Boers.

He talked about the huts his family lived in, of the beauty of his homelands and of the wild animals roaming free over mountains and plains. He said the fierce rhinoceros charged if you got too close to her baby calf. He described the wonder of the grand

14

eland grazing with ears twitching off flies and listening for leopards. He said the bulls locked large spiral horns and fought for the prize of an ewe. The following spring the hills were alive with calves no more then two feet at the shoulder who twitched and ran after their mothers at any sign of danger. Sometimes Tom told of a wily old leopard that stalked the ridges and sprang upon unsuspecting calves that had strayed from their mother. He explained that in nature every animal had to face danger and fight for survival.

Because Peter was a boy Tom gave him a tribal name. He called Peter uMgungundlovu or Elephant because he wanted Peter to grow to be big and strong. Louisa gave me my name, Studla, a Tswana name chubby, cuddly one.

With tears in her eyes, Louisa would tell us about her two small children who lived near Rustenburg a hundred kilometres away with her mother. She often spoke about how she missed them. 'If I didn't need money I'd be with them. I stay because of this, and so you poor tortured children have someone who cares.'

She said her children spoke, smiled, sang and danced or roamed the compound with friends. She'd tell us of how her people built houses out of mud and straw. There was no running water or electricity on her allotment and it took forever to find firewood, build a fire and make dinner. She ended these stories with how wonderful food cooked in the open in clay pots tasted. 'Like manna from God to give my children strength.' Finally, she would sing a song about the months of the year and count on our hands how long until she could take a holiday, go home and be with ones she truly loved. 'In my family we don't fight. Our time together is too precious. Oh how I wish your family were like mine. May God help you children.'

We loved these stories and these people. I think back often if Tom and Louisa had not offered us such love and acceptance our lives would have been bleak indeed.

School beginnings

By the time I went to school Peter, my baby brother, could read. I couldn't. My first teacher was a gentle lady who wore soft pleated tweed skirts and neatly buttoned shirts, Her black shoes were laced and she wore stockings, something Mum never did. Her grey hair was tied up in a bun and she smelled of rose petals. She was kind, thoughtful and took great care with each child. She quickly became aware of my special learning and emotional needs. I stayed close and she was kind when I stayed back in class during breaks to avoid the playground bullies. When I arrived, one day with a ten-pound note taken from Dad's wallet to spend at the tuck shop she rang my parents. 'Mrs. Wheeler suggests that we give you pocket money and we spend more time together Jilly Ponks. Would you like that?'

My second grade teacher was tall, thin, wore gym shoes, a ponytail and was good at sport. At break, she would run up and down the netball court blowing her whistle and holding her arms out to tell the bigger girls where to stand and what to do.

She had a sharp voice 'stand in line and put your shoulders back.' I didn't like her. We had to raise our hand, stand to answer questions and for reading, come out in front, and read loud to everyone. This was impossible for me. Letters would jumble together on the page and refuse to form words. I was totally illiterate. In terror of being exposed to my classmates, I began hiding in the toilet during reading lessons crouched on the toilet in a locked stall and wish 'let me read like my brother Peter.'

But my reading deficit continued, and I couldn't hide forever. One morning a freckle-faced, red haired, whining, teacher's pet named Simon yelled out 'Miss, Jill never does reading. It's not fair!'

'Jill, please come out to the front. Can you read for us?' the teacher asked. I struggle up, put one foot in front of the other. The air like warm syrup inhibited any movement. As I reached the front and turned to face the class, a sea of sneering faces stared back at me. I grasped the book shoved into my hands and tried to focus. I wasn't sure if it was right way up so searched frantically for a picture to orient the pages.

Then Simon laughed and my teacher sighed. 'Come on Jill. Do you know where we are?' The faces blurred and my knees trembled. There was no way I was going to get out of this stifling, claustrophobic classroom. So I tried.

But standing before the class my secret was immediately exposed. I was holding the book upside down and I couldn't read a word. The laughter is what I remember, especially after I cried and wet my pants.

'Quiet! Jill . . .' the teacher began, but I was already running, out of the classroom, down the corridor, through the courtyard, across a netball field and into a hedge. I cringed and choked for air, red faced with humiliation. I hated my teacher, Simon, Mummy, Daddy, Peter, anyone and everyone for my failures.

From then on, the bullies had a new name for me. 'Miss Piss!' they would cry as I rounded a corner or crossed the playground. Simon had started with 'Stand up straight Miss Piss' as I joined the back of line for class the morning after my reading debacle. Everyone laughed. I looked at my feet and wept. My new name spread like wild fire through the school. 'Miss Piss can't read, and wets herself in class,'

I tried dodging school. After breakfast, when I needed to leave, I would hide beneath the workbench in the tool shed, sobbing quietly. Under Louisa's bed or crouched double with my tear stained face against my knees in Russell's favorite nest. This hide out at the back of the house was cozy, dusty and the bushes tickled. Here I felt safe because it was out of sight behind the kitchen wall with no windows. But Mum always found me and insisted I attend. She was not sympathetic. Grabbing me by my ear or hair 'You know I go to work. You are so fucking selfish. If you can't handle a bit of teasing you will not survive? Now get out of here.'

I went. But by playtime, the horrors of my classmates teasing had sapped my strength. I found a hiding place in a tall hedge alongside the change rooms and close to the oval far from our classrooms and out of sight. Grade twos didn't go there. The hedge was about half a metre deep with tiny close-growing deep green leaves and lots and lots of branches. It was hard to get into at first but once I broke a pathway in it was easier to negotiate. There I'd stay watching from behind the thickest, scratchiest branches until the bell rang. Only once the last student had straggled inside, and I was positive the teacher was back in control at the front of the class, would I creep back. For grades two and three I was terrified, miserable, ashamed, and a quasi-truant, learning nothing at all. Nothing, except how to cry so quietly the tears stay on the inside, and how to be so still when others were around that I avoided notice.

Then, in my fourth year, Peter turned six and started school. Soon, all the teachers knew his name. Peter was the child genius who understood everything. One day he brought some wires, batteries and a jar of salt water to school and set his experiment up on a wall next to the playground. Crowds of kids jostled each other to watch on. He collected the hydrogen and lit it with a match. A teacher arrived on the scene just as it went pop. Excited, he steered Peter off to discuss science. The other kids were more than impressed.

Peter's popularity improved my social standing. Kids from the whole school suddenly wanted to know me. They'd ask 'How does Peter knew so many great experiments and his stories! Wow!' When they asked about science or the moon, stars and space I was completely flummoxed. Now Peter had their attention as well. Overnight, the bullying stopped. Mum had instructed me to watch over my little brother at school but in truth, he took care of me. During play and lunchtimes, I was always at his side. I watched as he played draughts or chess with older boys and pretended they were my friends.

Peter thrived at school intellectually, while I continued to struggle. Though I followed stories, accumulated some verbal knowledge, and even managed the occasional sum, the written words continued to blur on the page. There was just no way to differentiate between p and b and d. These all looked exactly the same to me and when I tried to write, I had the same ball at the end of a stick. I was quite good at keeping between the lines but I didn't use my right hand. So, all in all I was simply slow and stupid.

But at least I stopped trying to avoid school, a result that put a merciful end to the regular morning conflict with Mum. Despite being three years older than him, I clung to Peter for support in a world where intellect had value, but shyness and vulnerability were cruelly exploited.

At home the relentless pressure of politics persisted.

'See the papers today? They found Mandela not guilty in his Treason trial but the bastards banned him anyway. With him under house arrest for ninety days at a time they may as well have locked him away for good. What the hell will happen next?'

'Why did they do that Dad?'

'Because he is 'Black', a lawyer and he asks tricky questions like why can't everyone vote?'

'What happens if you can't vote?'

'Without a vote you're done for. It used to be special jobs for 'Whites' now it is wrong for a 'Black' man to shop at the same counter or sit on the same park bench or live in the same parts of town as 'Whites.' The Nationalists are getting more and more like the Nazi's. Soon they'll believe that 'Blacks' shouldn't even live in our country.'

There was no space for my problems. The family was consumed either with Dad and Mum's fighting or their lamenting the relentless build up of racism. Not only were there 'Whites' and 'Non-Whites', but 'Non-Whites' could be 'Blacks', 'Indians' or 'Coloureds'. If you were Chinese you were sometimes a 'Non-White' and if Japanese you were usually an 'Honorary White'. I was a Jew and Jews were 'White' but our taunts were generic: 'Kaffirboeties', the brothers of heathens, and 'Jewboys'. As Jews, we were assumed to be 'lefties' obliged to gift our spare time to holding the Nationalists accountable for what they saw as their God-given 'right' to dominate the blacks.

We continually talked about South Africa's institutional racism. Each mealtime we discussed the next nail in the coffin of Apartheid. These times were seldom temperate but occasionally they were agitated rather than angry.

'I can't live here. Verwoerd bloody 'Bantustans' - separate but equal.' Mum's voice would become almost hysterical. 'It's Hitler's work camps recycled. Move families into barren hellholes. Force them to work as migrant workers in order to send a pittance back to keep their families alive. This country is going to hell. Another Holocaust? How can anyone live with these fucking pass laws?'

'With Mandela banned, his African National Congress will go underground I'm sure and with those damn pass laws restricting people's movement they certainly won't stop opposing the Nationalists. Soon we'll see violence. It's inevitable. So much for pacifism.' Dad would take his head in his hands close his eyes and groan.

'You brought me to this God forsaken country?' Mum shrieked.

'I didn't! Remember. I came. You followed!'

'Bastard!'

'Yes Dear!' His sarcasm cut the air and Peter and I'd draw breath and wait. This might trigger a never ending cycles of anger and mayhem. Walking on eggshells I'd wait for the horror of past and present, to explode, while Peter retreated into his airplane and I sat alone frozen in terror.

***

Very occasionally Mum and Dad just did politics together. While Mum's party was on the far left believing in 'one man one vote' and Dad supported a more 'qualified franchise' based on education. They worked together to support friends trapped by the Apartheid system.

Sam Khan the leader of the Communist Party of South Africa was elected to Parliament in 1949 but expelled three years later under the Suppression of Communism Act of 1950. A close friend, he introduced my parents to many others of similar political persuasion. The Nationalist government believed that anyone who supported the 'Non White' cause 'was a Communist' likely to devastate the 'White' nation chosen by 'God' to rule their land. When Sam and other ANC sympathisers were banned in the mid-1950's my parents became involved in helping Sam and others escape the country.

Our outside rondavel, a guest room, often housed friends and friends of friends. All were political because in South Africa politics intruded into everything but not everyone was banned. And because my parents needed to keep the activity of some guests clandestine they'd be cagey about who stayed and why some disappeared in the middle of the night. This raised Peter's and my curiosity and added to the tension.

One morning I went to the rondavel, Peter close behind and peeped over the top of the closed bottom half of the door. 'Who are you and what're you doing here?' Panic ensued as a half dressed man unlatched the door, pushed past me, leapt over the side fence and dashed away before I could raise the alarm. Mum yelled and I ran to Louisa's room in tears.

That night Dad sat me down and said that it was imperative that I didn't go near the rondavel. 'When visitors come, you must leave them alone. Ask no questions.'

'But Uncle Jannie spoke to me.'

'Well it's different if they come into the house.'

'OK Daddy.' I didn't understand and neither did Peter.

Many years later Dad explained the strangeness of those very surprising instructions.

Dennis comes to dinner

Sometimes mum liked us to keep out. 'You'll eat supper in your room today. It's important for Dad and me to have times to enjoy our friends without you, and tonight I'm having a dinner party and want you out of our way.'

Flurries of activity fill the afternoon, Louisa and Tom take a break to wash and dress because tonight they'll be serving our special guests. Louisa wears her dark blue uniform and a bright white apron instead of her normal pink pinafore and Tom his pants and a white shirt instead of overalls. Mum goes into the kitchen, takes down her hand-written cookbook and tells us not to disturb her. She's seldom in the kitchen because it's Louisa's job to cook but she enjoys making special dishes. She announces that she'll be preparing two courses for the evening's meal and promises to give us a little bowl of '*Moren schnee*' a German chocolate delight with heaps of cream, if we're good.

We head outside, keeping clear of preparations until bath time. We wash, dress in pajamas, eat in my room and enjoy our desert. Then before sunset, we are tucked into bed. 'Keep out of the way, tonight is for grown ups only.' Peter reads and I look at books and draw.

We lie quietly for ages but eventually get tired of bed. We creep onto a balcony and out into the garden, shutting the door behind us so that that our escape won't be noticed. We discuss options and end up behind Louisa's room, where there's an old rope swing. We climb on to the plank tied by a knot through its centre and take turns to wind the rope up tight and letting go. First we turn fast then lean out from the centre. As the rope winds down our turning slows. Usually Louisa only allows us one or two turns but this evening they're not watching so we take turns until we are both so dizzy we cannot stand. We crawl onto the grass and laugh joyously at the strange giddy feeling. Lying flat on our backs, we look up the sky and watch the slow change from daylight into afterglow and then darkness.

Peter talks about the stars and I hum quietly and listen half-heartedly to his serious chatter. 'You know Venus is the evening star and Mars is the planet most like ours but did you know that Saturn's moons circle it just like our moon does.' As the evening chills we move back to our bedroom door. It's locked so we have no choice but to enter through the kitchen or lounge – both entrances that ensure the adults will see us. I worry knowing Mum will catch us. We go back to my window wondering whether Peter can squeeze through the burglar bars but I'm terrified he'll get stuck and cause more disruption then a simple dash through the living room.

Decision made. Peter goes to the front door because adults like him and I creep in through the kitchen and back into my room while the guests are distracted. The plan works superbly and because people love talking to Peter. I'm asleep by the time he comes back.

Later that night I wake, head and stomach throbbing. Despite two blankets, I'm shivering. I get up, go to the toilet and throw up, clean up the bathroom and shivering in the corner for ages scared to disturb Mummy when she's having her party. Finally, I'm feeling so sore and scared that I decide I need help, go into the lounge and stand shivering at the door. Eventually Dennis, one of mum's climbing friends, sees me. 'What's the matter Jilly?'

Mum turns, sees me and is immediately irate. 'I told you not to disturb us. What is it?'

'I'm sick.' I shiver and Dennis puts his hand to my forehead.

'I think she has a fever.'

'Jill go to bed. I'll attend to you later. Bloody kids always want something.'

Dennis puts his hand on my arm and steers me towards the hearth next to his chair. The fire is warm and welcoming. 'Sit a while Sweetie.' to mum, 'She's fine here with me. Not in the way. Are you, Jill?' Mum shrugs and turns away and Dennis strokes my hair as I sit at his feet looking into the fire. He brings me water and I drink. I listen as the grown-ups talk and think, why can't my Mummy be like Dennis?

23

Mountain Tragedy

Almost every weekend our family headed for the mountains. Here we met others, walked, camped and my parents climbed. As members of the Mountain Club we joined most official outings and when the club had no official outing Mum and Dad would camp with a core of long standing friends.

This eclectic mix included Harry the lawyer always upright, pompous and strong. He wrote the words we sang to 'When the moon above the ridges' and set it to the music of a traditional Anglican hymn. He expected his gentle red-haired wife Margo to stay home and love and nurture him and their children. She baked beautiful cakes and brought them to the mountains in a large green cake tin. Harry knew everything and was very important. He wrote a lot of the rules for the mountain club because he knew officialise. Margo's snuggles were very cuddly.

Bob an engineer knew everything about bridges and his wife June was tall and spoke quickly. Her children Tom and Jenny were little, very naughty and sang out of tune. I didn't like them because they told tales. Eddie was Swiss, as round as a ball, had an engineering business and made important stainless steel things. His wife Gladys was glam and didn't come to the mountains because there wasn't a bathroom so she couldn't keep clean. Dennis was divorced, I don't know what he did but he used to slap Mum on the bum and tell her to get off her high horse. Rex was a bachelor and didn't climb. He was always at our house. He was with Dad in the war in North Africa and taught him about English writers. Mum said 'he worked very hard at Anglicising us. Without him my English would still be 'sheit.' Emil a diamond cutter from Frankfurt spoke only broken English. The younger crew who hadn't married or had children yet included Miriam the doctor and the older ones like Sir Evelyn and an Afrikaans stoker and a plumber but enough for now.

All submitted themselves to the club rules for safe and cooperative enjoyment of their dangerous sport. They were my extended family. While I hated camping and seldom enjoyed the physical exercise, I was at home with the climbing mob. No one judged me. I could walk beside or sit quietly and cuddle up close to adults less self-absorbed then Mum and Dad. While Mum laughed with friends, ranted about how South Africa replicated the horrors of Germany or flirted with the latest good looking hunk and Dad either placated, ignored or remonstrated with his 'wild one from the Kameraden' Peter and I had company. Here we didn't have to hide.

On long weekends members would go further afield. In the winter of 1958 the club met at Kransberg about three hundred kilometres north of Johannesburg. Only one non-member came along, an Englishman called Martin. This well planned official camping trip is etched in my mind. It changed my life forever.

I was happy to go because for once we camped close to the cars. The usual routes took at least an hour of hard slog but in this big country we just wandered for half an hour through waist high golden grass to the base of the mountain.

I sang to myself as we walked, practicing variations on a theme to 'In the jungle the mighty jungle.' I would try and get the old fuddy-duddies to sing it around the campfire that night.

We camped in a gully running down from the rock face that stretched for hundreds of metres below an electric blue sky. This vertical rock wall was imposing and almost sinister and had a reputation for swallowing men. Only one steep ravine allowed access from the summit back to the foot of the cliff.

In the late afternoon, the mountain casts a vast shadow across the foothills adding an eerie suspense to the massive panorama. Only the brave tackled this edifice.

For this official outing, clear instructions were issued. Only the strong resilient climbers should attempt conquering this bastion. No trippers would be tolerated. The old hands were wary and reluctant about Martin's inclusion.

At night around the campfire, the conversation inevitably turned to politics. 'Bram Fisher is up to his neck in the treason trials and Mandela and the ANC are in trouble. I wonder what we're in for now?'

Dennis responded 'But did you see his new wife Winnie? Gorgeous hey?'

Dad immediately brought the conversation back to politics 'I'm worried about our country blowing up. The Nats will never allow equal rights so how long before the ANC give up on passive resistance and go for their Kalashnikovs?'

'Not long now! They can't be gentlemen forever. Not against such bastards.'

'Well it's their country too.'

'Tell Verwoerd and his bloody Nationalists that!'

Martin the intruder said 'Not interested in politics' and the old guard turned on him. 'You know nothing you slimy Pommy bastard.' They despised this man with his 'newfangled climbing ideas, shiny clanging equipment' and his talk of escaping the little woman and three kids to go climbing. 'The sort of loudmouth showoff the club can do without.'

Martin woke early despite a night of drinking, 'I'm off to add another ascent to my list. Who will second me?'

Dennis immediately intervened 'You drank too much last night.'

'I always drink and climb. Now who will second me or do I climb alone?'

Dennis was insistent this time 'You know the rules. No one climbs alone!'

'Oh for fuck's sake. Let's bloody go.' Always the first to resist authority Mum strode off and Martin picked up rope, slings and pitons, clattering as he rushed after her. Dad yelled, 'Else you're mad.' Dad knew he could not stop Mum.

People around the camp shrugged and turned back to their breakfasts.

Late morning, I heard a chain of urgent calls back to the camp.

'Cooee! Man down.' Everyone rushed to the bottom of the ravine, the only easy descent from the cliff face. Here a few metres into the wooded crevice Martin lay broken and bloodied on the ground. He'd fallen thirty metres and looked dead. Bob pushed away some undergrowth, went to Martin's side and took his pulse. June pressed closer, saw Martin and cried out 'Where's Miriam, we need a doctor.'

26

'He's breathing, we don't need to resuscitate but don't move him. His spine, we need to keep him still. Dennis, Paul a stretcher.'

Peter and I had rushed up with the others who'd been sitting in the stream not far below. We looked on but said nothing scared but knowing now was not the time to speak. Margo who'd been at the stream with us, found Miriam. 'She'll be here soon. Can we do anything to make Martin more comfortable?'

'No. He's unconscious but breathing. Leave him be.'

Dad pulled Mum away from the group and asked 'What happened?' She was ashen and visibly shaken, 'He refused to put in any piton or sling, said he'd show you patronizing creeps what could be done. I had no way of breaking his fall. I tried but he was twenty metres above me with the rope coming straight down with no break point, so when he slipped . . .,' Mum gasped for breath tears streaming down her check '. . . no sling, nothing held the rope, no way to help.'

'Else . . . calm down!' Dad steadied Mum. 'You should have said something to him!'

'I did! He didn't listen. What the hell could I do?' Mum shrieked. Miriam arrived and stroked Mum's arm as she passed. 'This isn't the time. Let's attended to Martin.'

Miriam checked Martin beginning by looking into his eyes and listening to his breathing, then with gently almost fluttering fingers felt her way down his body. She asked Bob to hold one of Martin's arms while she examined his chest taking particular care not to twist his body. 'He's unconscious, breathing is shallow we'll need to move fast.' With voice lowered, she turned to all of us and described what was needed. She took charge and we rushed to the tasks assigned.

Clambering over boulders and branches we cut down saplings took slings and karabiners and built a stretcher. With almost no word, Martin was carefully lifted, head held steady and placed on it. He uttered the quietest moan as he was lifted. Miriam took her place at his side; each man took up his position, hoisted the stretcher to waist height and slowly carried Martin down the mountain. Dad was at the front of the stretcher, face hard he looked strong and determined. The women, including Mum who was still crying, moved ahead clearing the path and stabilizing rocks for Martin's decent.

At the doctor's bidding a forward party rushed to the cars and on to the closest hospital thirty kilometers away and returned with several bottles of plasma. About a third of the way down the steep path the stretcher was lowered carefully, held horizontal and Miriam put a drip into Martins right arm. Again, each man took his turn to carry, one at the back the other in front as the party slowly snaked its way down the endless scree.

A hundred metres separated those clearing the path ahead of the stretcher and those at the rear. Everyone fully focused of his task. For a couple of hours the party quietly picked its way across difficult terrain towards the cars. Peter and I, the only children, were at the back carrying the equipment set aside by those who carried the stretcher.

Then, without a word spoken, the whole rescue team let out a collective sigh. We looked at each other and up at the endless blue sky. It was as if we could see Martin's spirit leave his body. Perhaps a sigh or a final exhale of breath. I can't explain but we all knew he was dead. We stopped looked at each other and nodded and then Dennis said 'His soul has left his body.' Miriam put her fingers on his pulse and confirmed our knowing. The procession now moved more quickly and without the quiet, reverent protection afforded Martin while alive.

At the car park, an ambulance awaited. Miriam climbed in alongside Martin's body and a policeman asked us to return to our camp and wait. We snaked back and quietly went about getting an evening meal ready.

This was difficult for me at the tender age of ten, and more difficult still for Peter at only seven. He looked at his food and I pushed my plate away and tried to hide my tears. We sat mute as people began to carp at each other. Bob kept asking 'What went wrong? We knew Martin wasn't up to it but we let him go.' Mum swore between her teeth 'It's my bloody fault but you bastards never gave him a chance. You were so fucking patronizing!'

Dad was really angry now. 'Else shut the fuck up. You've caused enough harm.' Recriminations kept coming until I finally slipped away, pulled my sleeping bag around me, and feigned sleep.

Next morning everyone packed up and Dad took Peter and me to the car ahead of Mum. She walked several steps behind talking to a policeman. When she got to the car, she got into the front seat and slammed the door. We crawled along for the first while but then picked up speed as we left the dusty farm road and joined the tar. Dad turned to Mum almost snarling 'Why did you allow him to climb so high without putting in a sling? Have you learned nothing? Why did you go with him when you knew he was hung over? Why, why why?'

I sat frozen next to Peter, heart pounding, feeling dizzy and couldn't focus. I wanted to throw up but was too scared to ask Dad to stop the car. I swallowed hard and looked at Peter. He chewed at his nails and stared out of the window. His knees were shaking just a little and he had goose bumps on his legs. Maybe he felt just as sick as I did. Finally, we get home and escaped to the kitchen where Peter and I cried into Louisa's chest.

This death became a sinister part of our life, an enormous stone in the gunnysack, a continual accusation, part of any argument and another rock to pull my parents' drowning marriage into the depths of despair.

Peter's response was to climb into his airplane and close the door. Now no one could reach him. He talked less, became less engaged with any outside interest and seldom smiled. He spent more and more time on his own. He continued to read and was still fascinated with anything scientific but he stopped including us in animated exchange. At home, he withdrew to his newly curtained off bedroom on the far side of the lounge and away from my parents or my bedroom.

Now Peter began to have two ways of being. At school, he was lively and engaged. He loved learning and showing others what he knew. He brought experiments to school and demonstrated to teachers and pupils alike. He explained the weather, how engines worked and talked about the extinction of the dinosaurs. He played chess with any comer and always won but at home when he was alone with Mum or me or with Dad, he disintegrated. He read more, drew, and wrote and sometimes he sat and stared. He was kind to me but distant and we didn't talk when we were sad.

My parents tried to reach Peter but his non-responsiveness scared them. Until Martin died, Peter always pushed to be heard but now it didn't matter any more. 'Dad and Mum are busy with Martin' he said and then turned away as did they. My parents were so caught in their spiral of accusation, blame and innuendo they didn't notice us. Their fiery feuds terrified me. Peter was in his airplane with its door firmly shut and I was alone and alienated so I turned away and faced my fears. The haunting nightmares became more present. I couldn't escape the Boogieman.

Finding a way to high school

In fifth grade, Mr. Ellis came to our school. Handsome, clever and a wonderful musician he came to work as a dedicated teacher with a special class of the eleven 'difficult' kids who could not read, write or do arithmetic. We spent all our school hours together and as a separate class, we worked at our own pace.

'I'm not interested in what you can't do. I want to learn everything about what you can. You've only got this year to prepare yourselves for high school. So let's get moving.'

We decided to put on a play. Mr. Ellis was encouraging but said 'you will have to learn lines, make costumes and work out how much money is needed for the materials to make them.'

First, we sat in a circle to tell each other our special stories. Amanda began and we all knew Cinderella. Once one fairy tale was told it was easy. Paul spoke about an ugly duckling and I cried because she reminded me of myself. Paul could quack very loudly and we all clapped when the ugly duckling grew into a beautiful swan. We liked this story very much but Jenny said duck costumes would be hard so we moved on to Sleeping Beauty. I told about 'Soupenkasper' who wouldn't eat his soup and went down the plughole. Tom didn't like it at all. He said it was too cruel. After two or three story-telling circles, each carefully shaped by Mr. Ellis who smiled, frowned or nodded and stopped any teasing, we decide to adapt Cinderella because everyone could dance or sing at the prince's ball.

We began writing the play with Cinderella, her two ugly sisters, her horrid step mum and the prince. We needed five more parts and decided that one would be the prince's manservant and each of the others would have a special act at the ball. Each character had a name and Mr. Ellis explained that characters are different from the actors who perform their parts. While we wrote we talked about how we were each different from the character we acted.

We talked about teasing and how hurtful it is. Told each other about our pain and how we would like others to see us. I found out for the first time that I was not alone in feeling hurt or ashamed. Finally, we were encouraged to boast about what we could do.

Some could hammer, others sew or dance and we used every one of these skills to enhance our production. Everyone was surprised that I could sing. Tom said he didn't even know I could speak because I always hid and never spoke in class. I was confident because of the harmonizing my family did when we were in the mountains or on long car trips.

But I had to prove it so with Mr. Ellis strumming on his guitar I raised my voice and filled the hall with the gentle sounds of a German lullaby and was rewarded with the part of Italian lady who sang the most important song at the ball 'Comma Prima.' Because my voice was good, Mary decided I needed to wear a Spanish comb in my hair. She had seen an opera singer with one. For the first time in my ten years, I asked Mum to take me to the Library. The Librarian helped me find the book and a picture of the comb. I pestered Mum until she bought me one and helped Tom weed the garden for a month to raise my half of the money.

We talked about who needed to work hardest on learning their lines and who would help with costumes and scenery. Mr. Ellis asked whether we could take the risk of inviting parents to help. We chose five mums to sew but helped with hems and buttons so I learned to thread a needle and sew a more-or-less straight seam. A few of the dads helped with the sets, though they were instructed to stick closely to our drawings and design.

Under Mr. Ellis' studied neediness, and our explaining each step we took, we blossomed. When I worked out that I could use arithmetic to estimate how much material I needed for my costume I was jubilant. I went home measured Peter, added a bit because I was bigger, chose the right sized pattern, read off the back how many metres of cloth I would need, multiplied this number by the cost per metre and told mum how much money was required.

Finally, the night of the performance came. I had only a few lines of dialogue but when I came to the centre of the stage and began singing I was rewarded with a sigh of delight from the audience. Everyone sat quietly listening, and all eyes were on me. My dress was beautiful and my hair piled high on my head secure with a glittering tiara. At last, I was on my own in front of an audience, and they were all on my side. The rapturous applause washed over and through me, filling me with confidence and pride. I looked towards the back of the audience and saw Mum, Dad and Peter clapping and enjoying a moment of pride rather than their usual disinterest.

Our play was a mammoth success. Chaotic perhaps with us all so eager to be seen that sometimes we came in ahead of cue but the whole school was there and everyone had fun. Parents and students all clapped wildly throughout the performance and at the end we sang several encores. What Mr. Ellis accomplished in his year with us was amazing. Many of us may have ended up in special schools or been kept down another year, but his enthusiasm had steered us to a place where we were now welcomed into high school. He had given us an opportunity to take the academic path.

My moment in the spotlight didn't solve all my academic or social problems. I still had a lot of catching up to do, with many years of crippling struggle with Janet and John in the first grade reader to come. I remained shy and constantly projected onto others the bad feelings I could not hold inside myself. I was still terrified of hoping for success because each past hope had been stillborn or overshadowed by Peter's brilliance. But thanks to a wonderful teacher who had faith that I could succeed, I had found that there is more than one way to learn. Through putting on Cinderella, I found I could absorb new information and, with this behind me, I was able to stay with my age cohort and the following year – 1958 – enter high school.

***

At home, things didn't change, 'Hans did you see the papers today? Verwoerd's arrested Mandela and sent him to Robben Island. No one stopped them. It Germany revisited. Soon none of us will be safe.'

'Well there are sanctions?'

'What are sanctions Daddy?' I'm not sure what sanctions are but more importantly will Mum and Dad talk or will this discussion end in a mighty fight.

'Sanctions are when other countries stop buying our products to make us change our politics and make Black people free.' Peter has read the papers and is fully informed and doesn't think this stuff will cause a fight. Why is it me who worries, and Peter who knows? Can't he see that Mum is about to blow up again?

'The ANC are organising a massive campaign and boycotts. This may help.'

'I guess starving us of petrol may make a difference but I'm pretty sure we're self-sufficient in most areas. We grow our own food. It'll make business hard if I'm cut off from my European suppliers but to the average man I don't think it will make much difference. Who knows?'

'That'll take forever. It's the bloody Holocaust again. We must leave.'

'And go where?

'I can't stay and face the hatred again! These Boers remind me too much of Hitler. Their bloody belief that God has chosen them, the Super race because they are white. Their ranting that blacks are the 'son's of Ham' born to serve, draw water and clear the land. It's just like Germany with their golden haired Hitler youth and Jewish vermin? I can't survive so what the fuck will you do about it? I can't live here, and what about your kids?' Mum is off again, her anger a distraction because fighting helps us forget the awful politics we cannot change.

34

This particular argument is vey confusing and both Peter and I are silent. Is anyone who is Afrikaans bad? We have neighbours across the vacant lot who speak Afrikaans and Mum calls them 'the chosen.' I like them because they laugh and sing and celebrate around their kitchen table. Their family is large. A grandma, a Ma and Pa, eight children, three dogs, numerous cats and most exciting lots of hens and a cockerel who wakes us each morning. They always say 'Come right in' and often ask Peter 'the clever little Englishman' and me to join them whatever meal they are having. 'There is always room for a couple of extra kids.' They say thank you to God for good food and health and Pa always says a special blessing for us because as welcome visitors. They don't seem scary. They never scream like Mum and Dad.

***

Despite the persistent backdrop of political pessimism, I was distracted in my last junior year. Focused on pulling myself together and preparing for high school I almost stopped worrying about Mum, Dad and Peter.

Mum loved my 'Comma Prima' and caught a glimpse of the spirited young woman I could become. She made an appointment with Mazy Wait an eccentric spinster who spent many hours wondering through the mountains with others from the club. While they climbed, Mazy sat below and sketched. She also enjoyed sketching the bodies of lithe young climbers sunning themselves around mountain pools. Her landscapes peppered with comical figures hanging from the cliffs by their fingernails were often used to illustrate the mountain club journals. Mazy worked as an art teacher at a private girls school. She and mum talked and without consulting me Mazy achieved the impossible and got me into this prestigious private school.

My life changed forever. My connection to classmates I had grown to trust while working towards joint outcomes in our play was lost as they went to the local government school up the road and I no longer saw them.

***

A prison can take on many forms and Kingsmead though beautiful became mine.

The grounds stretched for a huge block on the East side of Oxford Road one of Johannesburg's most select thoroughfares.

The generous tarred driveway was hidden from the perimeter wall by lovely trees. Entry through a stone gateway allowed perhaps seven chauffeured Mercs to stop in line and spill out lovely, precocious girls at one drive through. From here, the lawns sloped gently to a grassed quadrangle surrounded by a substantial double storied stucco building shaped in a U.

The main offices, hall, library and classrooms nestled into the grounds to the left. Ahead lay a permeable block of toilet facilities below a second story of boarder's dormitories. To the right was a large glass-walled dining room where each scholar must lunch and learn the etiquette of a young lady. Beyond this gracious U lay many sports fields, tennis courts, a chapel, swimming complex and more classrooms. All were well maintained, generous and well appointed.

My new high school was tailored to winners. The parents of these young ladies had reserved their places at birth and their education was meticulously planned to shape the future leaders of South African society. Teaching standards were high and critical thinking was encouraged with a place for debate in every class. For the first time I listened to political argument rather than being spoon-fed a one-sided view of history. This strengthened my political convictions and prepared me for holding my ground against opposition. Mathematics and science were taught at the highest level and all pupils had to learn a language other than English and Afrikaans. Kingsmead was simply 'among the best schools in the English-speaking world.'

Every aspect of academic learning, sport, religious education and even deportment was significant in raising well-rounded young women ready for the world and each student was continually monitored.   Still unable to read I was now ranked in every endeavor and found wanting at every turn. I even failed deportment called back after gym 'Jill your posture is poor. You slouch and hold yourself badly. Put your shoulders back and look at those you converse with? A large bust is nothing to be ashamed of and if you are overweight watch your diet. You are letting your team down again. Surely in this at least you can try harder.' At the end of each term I would get the lowest score possible and Mum would yell. There was only one hope my voice. I could sing.

***

By the end of term one I had a small circle of friends, all misfits. Anneke's mother and father were divorced, almost unknown in the fifties, and she was hurt and angry. A gifted guitar player and artist she wanted nothing more than acceptance but this was not forthcoming from the first form. Jenny a petite dancer wanted to go to the Royal Academy of Dance and not to study. This obsession earned her banishment from the studious crew. Viv had Maori blood and was very beautiful. She was tall willowy, honey-skinned and full of life and laughter but somehow she was not ladylike enough to find acceptance. My only skill was singing but my capacity for self-deprecation and cynicism earned my spot in the disgruntled four. Together we stood our ground by finding as many antisocial exploits as our pre-pubescent minds could generate. We were late for classes, hid behind the change rooms while Viv smoked, and the rest of us coughed. Sometime we did the unforgivable, leave school for the lunch break and go to the local shopping centre. On a couple of occasions, we stole small items of clothing from a boutique across the road. On one jaunt, Viv shoved her school uniform into her satchel and left the shop in two layers of stolen clothes. It was hard to hide our laughter that day. When these exploits attracted little attention, we became more brazen in our acting out but with little recognition. There was just no way any girl from our school could do such things and of course, there was an entire underclass to shoulder such recrimination. White girls from posh schools simply did not steal.

***

On an early Monday morning in my second term, the entire school is assembled for singing practice and prayers. Our group hangs out at the back of the hall. We have separated ourselves form our form who sit in front of the auditorium in three neat rows. We won't conform. Two climb on the bars. Jenny demonstrates the third ballet position and Viv mimics her. Anneke and I crouch out of sight behind the jumping horse just in front and to the right of the bars and giggle. Before we know it there is an imperious demand from the front. 'Will the girls who

37

are giggling stand up now!' I wink at Viv, suppress my laughter and jump to attention.

Miss Rawlings a grey haired wizened old music teacher points at me and says 'Well you are clearly proud of your voice so sing me the first two verses of the school song.' Without a second thought, I raise my voice, fill the hall with my rendition of 'Praise our Lord the King of heaven', and then bow to the thunderous applause of all assembled.

I even turn the teachers my way. 'What a wonderful voice you have' concedes Miss Rawlings. 'Go and join the choir in the gallery. Now.'

I join the choir as an alto and Anneke soon enlists. We are early for every practice as we both love singing and the recognition and acceptance that come with belonging. The following year the school decides to perform Mozart's 'Marriage of Figaro' and I am picked for a substantial solo part. I'm excited and rehearse often. Perhaps too often because I get a raw throat and am advised to stop singing until it heals. It does not and I am hospitalized and have my tonsils out.

The operation is unsuccessful, my voice box is damaged during surgery, and when I come out of the anesthetic, I'm in great pain. I cannot speak at all for several days and am fed through a tube because I can eat nothing. I'm sedated to stop me pulling at the tubes used to drain the suppurating sores in my throat and larynx. When I'm finally released Mum tells me that the surgeon says I must not speak or sing for at least six weeks. I mope around at home for a couple of weeks with no voice at all and then return to school but without energy. I cannot speak above a whisper never mind sing and my newly found entrée into the schools elite evaporates. I blame the damn music teacher Miss Rawlings. She made me join the choir and gave me false hope.

I go back to the choir and watch my understudy practice and then sing in my place. She is wonderful and I am devastated. I become depressed and can find no enthusiasm for school. As I lose hope of achieving in any realm, I begin to project my failings onto others and despite encouragement from Phenella, my lovely young choir mistress, leave singing and retreat into the comfortable shapeless cover of the overlooked outsider. I hang back disheartened and lost. Having no confidence to stand my ground I face long tedious days isolated, bored and adrift.

In the summer break I spend endless hours alone in my room. School is shit, Peter distant and Annie my only real friend has her own stuff. While we talk on the phone and see each other, this doesn't break the tedium.

I almost enjoy my melancholy. I spend hours glued to my peppermint green transistor radio, learn to love Elvis Presley and dream about him leaving me lost and alone as he finds a better girl. I sulk around all day and at night I hide in my bed. The Boogieman returns.

Sharpeville another trauma

Dad always said politics is personal. 'Before Hitler my family had nothing to eat. Hyperinflation overwhelmed us; Germany borrowed money to repay their WWI reparations and the paper Marc became utterly worthless. People took wheelbarrow loads to buy a loaf of bread. It was so bad that I scrabbled through dustbins for potato peelings for us to eat.'

Hitler blamed the spiralling unemployment of the Great Depression of the 1930's on the Jews. In South African where only whites voted, the Afrikaners blamed the 'non whites' for stealing their jobs. The Nationalist government proclaimed the Urban Areas Act in 1923 banning 'native' men, women and children from entering cities unless the whites needed their presence. This continued until 1934 when Jan Smuts and his newly elected government became less rigid in enforcing segregation.

In 1936 my parents were among the 2,500 Jews welcomed as refugees to South Africa and during their first years of settlement they didn't worry about racism. However towards the end of WWII fear of racial assimilation built again among the whites and led to the defeat of Smuts and his United Party in the year of my birth 1948. Mum often said 'You were tiny and premature because I was terrified when the Nationalists won that racism would spiral out of control in South Africa as it had in Germany.'

She was right as the new government immediately began to work on apartheid. Now pass laws demanded that 'black' people carry passbooks when outside their homelands or designated residential areas. Failure to produce a pass resulted in arrest and any 'white' could ask a 'black' to produce their pass.

Dad talked long and often about fascism as the cancer that stole his youth. 'Hitler was the malignant tumour, who brought your mother and me together in the Kameraden. In this Jewish youth group we committed ourselves to fighting fascism in whatever form it took.'

'I know Dad.'

'That's why we came here. We shared the same history; we had camped and climbed together and learned about political resistance.'

'Yes Dad'

'I became a pacifist. That's why I joined the South African air force as a navigator in the North Africa to support those who fought German fascism without taking up arms myself. This same fascism destroyed democracy in South Africa, traumatizing us all. It's shaken your mother's sanity, got her drinking and enraged me.'

'I know Dad.'

'This cancer fuelled our family feuds and affected you. Your mum wanted to leave but where to go. So we supported the ANC in their peaceful resistance and then finally there was Sharpeville in 1960.'

***

Pass laws became more and more restrictive and the ANC finally suggested that all blacks simply burn their passbooks. Things were electric and our family was vigilant.

At home Tom and Louisa asked for earlier hours and my parents happily complied. 'We want to be in our rooms with the doors locked before dark. There're too many questions about passes and people want us to join the protest.'

'Of course! Wash the dishes in the morning but if you wish to join the protest do. We'll support you.'

'Thank you Boss'

'Don't call me Boss. I'm like you no more.'

Dad was abreast of all political activity, obsessed with the papers and read us snippets each night,

The ANC is running a peaceful protest. They are asking people to burn their passes quietly at home and then insist on being arrested if they are challenged by the police. They must simply say, 'You can't arrest us all.'

Everyone began listening to the news and our family reacted as they always did. A replay of old times.

Dad said 'I am scared the Nationalists will overreact. Look what happened in Germany and there Jews were compliant.' Mum reacted on cue.

'How many times must we face Fascism?'

Dad took the bait 'And what should I to do about it?' Peter, keyed to blow, disappeared, his frantic humming echoing the mood. I muttered to myself 'Oh hell Peter keep it together, there's enough going on. I need you.' After dinner I went to bed with my transistor radio but couldn't find a station mentioning the strike. This built my anxiety.

A couple of days later we heard the first tales of disaster. Sabre jets were flying over Sharpville. Everyone in their path was terrified by this thunderous demonstration of power.

We had no television and while news travelled quickly, the true picture built slowly. The first was that in Sharpeville, a newly built township, ANC organisers decided to move beyond the quiet protest. They held a rally, build a bonfire, burned their passes in public, and then marched to the police station and demanded to be arrested.

And then on the 21st March 1960 Dad threw down the Star. A huge banner headline read **'7,000 march through Sharpeville 250 dead or injured'** and proceeded to tell us the story. 'When the blacks took their passes to the municipal offices about 300 policemen came with five Saracens. They didn't ask the crowd to disperse they just strolled around showing off their rifles. Then a policeman said 'Fire' and mayhem ensued. All the blacks ran; well those who were not shot or injured.

'The Government is responsible, it's their damn 'pass laws'. Now those who oppose apartheid will take up arms. Now every peaceful method has gone only violence is left.

From then on Dad searched out every article on Sharpeville. We discussed nothing else for months. He kept reading clippings over breakfast and dinner. He started a scrapbook and mumbled to himself about keeping an account of what was happening. Mum yelled 'Must we hear every bloody blow. I am beside myself, Peter is disappearing . . .'

I listened to Mum and watched Dad. Hope for our country was running out, but more important my family would truly disintegrate if Dad's hope were extinguished. He had always believed it was his job to steer us through political turmoil and the resulting trauma. If he stopped trusting himself there would be nowhere to hide and no hope of survival.

Mum paced and yelled incessantly, stopped work for several weeks, moped about and planned a trip to Europe saying she would leave this bloody country and us. Dad said nothing. Peter withdrew. His only comment 'Your fighting has nothing on those Nationalist madmen. Well now you both have something to blame for the hell you make us live in.' I gasped at his audacity.

At first I couldn't talk about what had happened. Raised to be sensitive to political issues, I was now convinced that South Africa was on a direct path to full-scale mayhem. Dad kept saying 'We are the world's pariahs.' He scared me and I felt completely abandoned to the mighty forces of political madness. I didn't know what to do. But within a couple of days I could bear this political oblivion no longer and turned again to my school failures. I had three friends but the teachers had it in for us, the downtrodden within my snobby school. Here I'd negotiate my own pass laws. 'God help me.'

After a couple of months things settled. Peter still hid in his room and mumbled, sung, analysed and planned. He watched Louisa, Tom and their friends and sometimes talked about our hopeless land South Africa, where people are judged by the colour of their skin and not by conscience. He steered clear of Mum and Dad. But storm-weathered he came out talking.

Dad and Mum told us they had talked through separation but come to the conclusion that they had been together while escaping one holocaust and could support each other through the next. 'We are Jews and some Jews are built to struggle, support the downtrodden and survive.'

And so despite my worst fears life carried on.

Re-finding my place

By second year of high school I was well and truly sick of well-heeled, confidant young ladies from settled upper middle class backgrounds. However it was a new year and my resolution was to find some way to fit in. I would not be a loser. It was just too boring so I girded myself and looked for new opportunities. Where would I start?

There were several cliques so I planned my attack. 'I should fit in with the Jews after all I am one.' I wrangled a visit to Hilda's grand house and stood on a wonderful Isfahan carpet in the centre of a huge entrance hall face turned up in awe as I drank in the beauty of a magnificent stained glass window stretching for a full two stories. It flanked a superb silver grey wooden staircase modern and spare. The whole room was suffused in a warm kaleidoscope of colours, light and ethereal. I had never been anywhere so beautiful.

This visit was astonishing. I spent the afternoon sitting with Hilda in her father's study. We sipped lemonade from crystal glasses and nibbled at biscuits of honey and almonds and listened as Mr Rebinowitz a formal Reformed Jew sat upright, his silk waistcoat buttoned, silver pipe in hand, and spoke of Jewish life and lore. About kosher food and burying crockery in the garden to keep it clean, about not bathing a calf in its mother's milk, about walking to schule and not working on the Sabbath. Then he turned to me and asked where my family hailed from and where we worshiped. When I said we did not, he pronounced 'then you are not a Jew.' After that I was excluded. I was not invited to sit with the Jewish girls and when I approached they titter about how I had no religion and no God. In class they were polite but there was no place for me among the kosher clutch of girls sunning themselves at recess. We shared the same holocaust and were granted the same respect in History class but this was where the similarities ended. My parents were non-believers; we didn't live in the high-class ghetto close to the schule. Hilda, Sue and Sally, Benita and Jane all with their big houses among their own, with successful professional parents, heaps of wonderful clothes and a religious identity, let me know at every opportunity that I wasn't like them and no amount of trying would grant me access. They were the chosen. I was not.

The Anglicans were at school because of church affiliations. Several came from big farm properties and loved their horses, riding, pony clubs and the church's youth community. Leanne led this select group. She directed their interest and developed an inner and outer circle of followers. To be an intimate there were fixed requirement. A good-looking older brother to help with study and play was a prerequisite. Leanne sat on the fire escape landing between the first and second floor and held court laughing and talking about older boys, hockey, jodhpurs and parties, parties, parties. 'Jane, who was that super guy you were with? He's not your boyfriend is he because I have to have a crack at him! Those blue eyes and he looks wonderful in his polo neck. I bet he can ride.' Leanne laughed and Jane turned away. I could see her blush from my vantage point way below and to the side of the fire escape. The colour rose on her neck and her cheeks went red.

Viv turned to me 'That bitch is at it again. Why doesn't Jane tell her to piss off and get her claws out of her boyfriend? I don't know what they see in Leanne.'

I nodded my head agreement but secretly I knew why Jane kept trying because I to would have done anything to be Leanne's friend. Everybody wanted to be part of her special crew. She was so cool.

Also she knew just how to make you cringe, a word from her and you were out. The other day at swimming Sue swam breaststroke in the crawl length and Leanne yelled for her disqualification. Sue was mortified. What a bitch. And in History she said it was clear that the 'blacks' just couldn't keep up. 'They have smaller brains. It's been scientifically proven.' I hated that stuff but hated more that others agreed and I didn't stand up to her because I just couldn't take her flack.

The in-groups had parties all the time but in truth I, as one of the also rans, went to an occasional event arranged by the less cool. Now, being invited was not enough. I wasn't good company, had little to boast about and nothing to trade, I wasn't a smiler and my small talk was non-existent. All in all I was no asset. I watched on as people turned their backs not in anger or disdain but almost in pity. Soon I was wiped from the list.

Apprehension built. I wasn't cool, I couldn't keep up in class and I had times when I couldn't even talk to the misfits. Hiding places were hard to find so I needed some way out of the mire of my own inadequacies. I tried fantasy. 'I read the new Dickens.'

'What new Dickens? My mother owns a bookshop and Dickens has been dead forever. Lying loser.'

I slunk off shamefaced. That didn't work so what now? I assessed my assets. There weren't many. I had big boobs but they made me look fat. I could play on sympathy by dragging Peter into the limelight but that was risky. I might be tarred with his madness or worse still laughed at because my family is mad. People already thought I was poor and lived in a third rate suburb. They had seen Mum hauling my bike from the roof rack of her Fiat 500 as they arrived in their chauffer driven Mercs and teased me about that already. Who knew what next?

The only asset others didn't have was the Mountain Club with lots of groovy older guys usually nice to me because they wanted something from Dad. For starters Philip always chatted to me despite him being three years my senior. He wore glasses and his Midlands accent was a little off putting but at least it wasn't Afrikaans and he was very kind. He talked about climbing, politics, God and family problems. Not his, mine. Good-looking in a bookish sort of way, bronzed because of his climbing, he had the most wonderful smile, full and generous and engaging. I was sure they'd love him, and there was also John and Simon and a couple of guys who had recently come from the Cape. They were all brawny and big and gorgeous and smart as well. They all went to university and could talk forever about anything. How could I get those stuck-up misses interested?

I went home and told Mum I must have a party and I needed her help getting some good-looking mountaineering guys to come. 'What happened?' To my surprise Mum understood. She recognized my agony at not belonging. She nodded as I talked about class cliques and particularly related to my distress at not being a good enough Jew. Teary, I spoke about my attempts to fit in. 'I miss Mr. Ellis's class and don't know how to be a lady.' Mum was uncharacteristically quiet. Then 'Sounds just like what happened to me in Frankfurt. Your grandmother always made

46

me spend time with the synagogue crowd but we had nothing in common. I hated listening to their pompous crap. 'Well you have a choice my girl. We'll show these stuck up young ladies there's more to lives than airs and graces. We'll have your party. A barbeque, music, dancing on the veranda and even a fruit crush with bitters and a small amount of wine to add a punch and of course lots of bona fide men. They'll see what real fun is! Their pretentions can't win against pure pubescent passion and the mountain club guys will get anyone going. Now where do we start?'

Mum got some pop music from friends. We planned a barbeque with an easy eat mountain meal and I got a new dress that Mum said she couldn't afford. 'Your bloody school costs so much and now a damn dress. When will it end? Oh well I guess there is no point in the school if you don't mix. Use this opportunity well. There won't be another.' My bright floral dress was blues and purple with tight bodice, filled to capacity by my big bosom and a wide gathered skirt over a flouncy white petticoat that swirled if I jived with enough gusto.

I invited my whole form but several girls declined. 'My mother would rather I didn't. We're not sure about your part of town. We never go past Parktown. Those newer suburbs have lots of public school kids and gangs hang out close to your house don't they? Anyway we're comfortable in our group but good luck. Have fun.' I was astounded that Leanne accepted until I heard her whispering loudly that she had to check my place out. 'I bet the guys are a figment of her imagination.'

The evening came. I waited anxiously by the window and watched for people to arrive. Peter laughed 'Don't worry Jill, I'll keep them entertained. Do any of them play chess?' Peter had a way of heightening my anxiety. He'd get more and more over the top. I knew he would. He'd show off and tell everyone about the universe or contradict someone and point out their error in an encyclopaedia or . . . My imagination running wild I wished he could be supportive instead of overwhelming. I added my fear of his eccentricity to my long list of watch outs and wished Mum had insisted on his sleeping over elsewhere. Dad was away as usual and I was truly terrified. I'd created my own demise. With Peter's help I'd be the laughing stock forever.

47

The gorgeous guys arrived together in two carloads. Philip my stalwart had brought Henry a good-looking redhead with bright blue eyes and a wonderful smile, John stocky and sandy haired and willowy Mike. The other car was full to capacity and I gasped in awe as, one after another, real men piled out and threaded their way down our path. Well who cared who came now? I'd be fully occupied just checking these hunks out. Thank God for Dad and his climbing reputation. My night was made. Each fellow introduced himself with a smile and went out onto our veranda where they chatted happily with any comer.

Annie arrived early, Viv and Jenny didn't come, but three other outcasts arrived. One I didn't know because everyone moved about between lessons depending on their capacity in each subject. Another hung around the periphery of our group. They tittered shyly as they arrived, moved outside and goggled at the talent. The groupies clearly curious dribbled in later. Their first overtures were condescending. 'What a lovely little cottage. So colourful. Where do you sleep?' When Leanne arrived, late she was gracious. 'Hello Jill it's lovely to be here, thank you. She turned to Rex who was there to support Mum in Dad's absence and smiled widely. 'Thanks for having me in your home. Is there somewhere I can put my bag?' Her mouth fell open as she moved onto the veranda and saw what I had on offer in the man stakes.

All of us girls were on our best behaviour because of the beautiful boys. I watched as my classmates laughed coquettishly, danced happily and surprise, surprise even included me in their chatter. As the evening progressed the party warmed up. The music was a little outdated but we all danced together a dipping, swirling mass. I loved my dress with its flouncy layers of petticoats swishing and swirling as I dipped and turned to the beat of 'Rock around the clock' and 'Jailhouse rock.' Everyone was up, laughing, singing and talking at the top of our voices. Mum rocked with the rest of us and as always her sleek athletic body looked wonderful as she writhed and shook with the best of us. Even Peter danced. I'd seldom felt so unselfconscious, alive, involved and happy. This was simple good-hearted fun. To my very great surprise the party was a roaring success. The hunks from the club had achieved what I

48

alone could not. They had brought out the best in everyone; the music was cool and the food to die for. I had a winner.

Well into the evening, some giant, greasy gatecrashers roared full throttle down our street on huge motorcycles, took off their helmets, swaggered down our pathway brushing their Brylcreemed ducktails away from their faces and hammered at our front door. In a flash Mum had gone. Someone on the veranda saw the intruders and alerted the rest of us. The mountain climbing hunks readied themselves to muscle in and evict the intruders but Philip raised his hand 'hang on.' My five-foot Mum appeared at the door, ice axe held high above her head. 'Bugger off!' We all goggled and gasped as the great big bikers gawked at her fierce flaming eyes, halo of wiry black hair, turned tail and slunk sheepishly out the gate, mounted their mighty iron steeds and whispered away. My reputation was sealed. I had the coolest parties. Now my position was forever secured. The whole school would hear about my legendary mother and everyone would know about my parties.

While I'd never be part of the cool crowd I'd had a definite win. I could pull guys and my mum was legend. Now hopefully not too many people would taunt me.

Whatever happened to Peter

After the mountain incident, trust in our family was shattered. Dad spent less time at home and when he did, my parents were angry. Dad continually blamed Mum for the accident. 'You've stolen my only retreat. You are never rational, you're mad!' Recriminations flew and there was less and less comfort in our home. Peter responded by talking less and eavesdropping more. When Mum and Dad argued, he retreated. Fights about money left him mumbling about how costs could be reduced or ways he could earn to cover expenses.

Perhaps the biggest change was that Peter completely stopped talking about his ideas. Now he simply went inside often talking or laughing to himself 'Well Peter what do you think about atoms . . . the encyclopedia says' and then he quoted - usually verbatim Dad told us. I heard him converse with my parent's friends, with Tom and Louisa, and at school. But he just didn't trust Dad, Mum or me any more. He choose this quiet, eccentric way for years while I slunk around consumed with not being able to read, hiding in the shadows and projecting my inadequacies onto others.

'Peter, help, I can't understand how this electromagnet works. I've got a drawing with arrows but I don't understand what current is or what magnets do.'

'Well look it up in the encyclopedia.'

'Peter you know I can't read!'

'No! I'm working on chess, light and Einstein. It's all relative you know.'

'Peter . . .' He'd turn from me, eyes hazed over as if he was no longer in the room with me. He simply wiped me from his presence. His mind disappeared and only his body was there.

In his last year of junior school Peter seldom smiled and he ate little. His form teacher confirmed our concerns saying 'Peter's unresponsive in class. He sits quietly at the back of the class and takes no interest in his lessons or his classmates. This is a very distinct change from the intelligent, inquisitive, lively and almost disruptive pupil of the past few years.'

Towards the end of year Mum took him to the doctor, worried that he was depressed. The doctor said Mum's concerns were premature. 'He is pre-pubescent. He'll grow out of it.'

Then suddenly he grabbed centre stage.

This memory stands out as clear as day. My parents were out for dinner. I sat cross-legged on the couch doing homework. Elvis Presley sang loudly from the forbidden radiogram. My vision was drawn to Peter now twelve. He huddled over a pile of clothes in the middle of Mum's favorite Persian rug.

'What're you doing?' Peter had a box of matches and reached towards his new school uniform a lighted match in hand. I ran at him yelling 'Stop!' His face contorted, he picked up the poker and I ran full pelt from the house Peter after me waving the poker. 'I'll get you. Don't interfere!' and then he shrieked like a wounded animal. I was terrified.

'Help!'

Tom and a friend rushed from Tom's room tackled Peter to the ground and used all their strength to hold him down while Louisa and I charged inside. The clothes were badly singed but not burning. We called and Mum and Dad hurried home. The doctor was there within minutes and tranquilized the still writhing and ranting Peter.

That night I lay shaking in my bed continually needing to pee. I just couldn't hold all my feelings inside. Each time I closed my eyes I saw Peter's wild face as he chased poker in hand, mouth open and eyes ablaze, howling like a hurt animal as he ran. I was falling apart. This was so hard. Who'd stop him? See me? How could I survive in this madhouse? A never-ending vortex drew me to its centre. I couldn't go on. I tried lying still and forcing myself to breathe but I couldn't. 'Somebody please help.' I fell asleep and as morning dawned and I got up, dressed asked Louisa for money and caught the bus and went to school. There was no talking to Dad or Mum today.

Once at school, I crept into the space below the stairs. In this small music room, seldom used, I dropped my bag and fell to the floor. I sobbed and sobbed. What was happening? Why did Peter do what he'd done? Nothing made sense. I sat here all day and after the final bell, I left, walked the long way home spent. Nothing mattered.

The fire episode was seen as an aberration, the second incident where Peter chased and stood over me with a carving knife was concerning and with the third, where Peter tried to cut the cat open, a pattern was established. Now Mum and Dad, also transfixed by fear, stood helplessly by as an unsure mental health system intervened. Peter was too young to be labeled and there were no prescribed methods for dealing with what he was doing. There were places and treatments for kids with physical or mental disabilities, ways of managing adults who had illnesses like depression or mania or schizophrenia, but nothing for a twelve-year-old boy who needed containment, diagnosis and treatment. Dad went from our family doctor to a psychiatrist and then to books on mental illness. Our doctor came home to consult my parents and I hid within earshot. Dad began 'There must be a solution. Others will have faced such problems.' The doctor shook his head.

'Peter is too young to be hospitalized. You will need to care for him at home. Perhaps he will calm on medication but this will take time. You will need to watch him.'

I crept into the room.

Mum yelled 'I can't stay home; I need to work to stay sane myself.'

Dad chipped in 'And the money I earn for the family is not important?'

'I can't control him and neither can you.' Mum turned to the doctor 'There must be somewhere he can go.'

The doctor looked at me and suggested that my parents find something else for me to do but my mother yelled. 'She's part of this bloody family. She knows what's going on. It's your bloody fault Hans. You're never here and you blame me for everything.'

'What about all your fucking around, your politics, your business. Everything you do is so important. Well he's your son so what the hell will you do.' The doctor stared at me and said nothing. He finally left but the fighting continued.

For weeks, Peter needed constant watching. Tom was often called in to help Dad constrain Peter who was as 'high' as a kite, like a motor running at three or four times normal speed. When he ate, he gulped down several plates of food without tasting. He stuffed the food into his mouth with his hands and gulped it down with his mouth open for the next handful. He didn't sleep, was overactive all the time, never sat still, weaved about the house and walked for miles and miles a day. He believed he could do anything but was absolutely and completely uncontainable.

I spent as much time as possible in my room, afraid. My parents kept pleading for medical help. They screamed, blamed, threw things, howled at their misfortune and finally accepted that their beautiful boy, their shining hope, had severe symptoms, possibly of schizophrenia and bipolar disorder. We could not reach him, medication didn't help and Peter needed shock treatment. This could only be done in a mental hospital for adults. Dad asked 'What are the side effects.'

The psychiatrist answered 'There are not many but most difficult is that when the brain is reset so to speak, short term memory is lost.'

Peter was removed and three or four weeks later, a burned out husk with vacant eyes, no voice, a shadow of Peter, shuffled back into the house. He remembered us but nothing of the past six months. He was now 'low' and moved about in slow motion, talked in a monotone, pushed his food around his plate and seemed to taste nothing. He didn't turn to face people who spoke and showed no interest things happening around him; his only sign of life was that he stroked his forearm as if he were feeling his skin to test if his body was alive.

My parents were told that we had now seen the highs and lows of manic depression but this wasn't Peter's diagnosis because the doctors had also seen symptoms of schizophrenia and it was clear that he sometimes heard and responded to voices in his head.

Once he was more or less stabilized, Dad went to Peter's school and asked his form teacher for help. Sympathetic he brought piles of books and papers to our home. Within a month, Peter had relearned what he'd lost; but just as we begin to hope, he slid into depression and wanted only to sleep or play his guitar. His soulful music echoed his despair. I looked into Peter's blank eyes. His life force could not push past the depression. It was happening again. The cycle was starting for a second time and I couldn't go through this again. I was terrified. I went to my room and wept, my heart broken.

Eventually Peter came back from his catatonic depression, was himself for an instant and then we all knew he would be high again soon. My parents phoned the psychiatrist, 'Peter is going high; he needs hospitalization now!'

'What has he done?'

Dad replied 'Nothing yet but the agitation is back.'

'Don't dramatize; you're overprotective.'

The police picked up a raving, disheveled and incomprehensible Peter that afternoon. 'He stopped the traffic by sitting in the middle of a busy intersection, refused to move and expected us to direct the traffic around him. When I said no he attacked me.' Peter was committed to the same hospital again and we mourned our impotence in the face of Peter's illness.

Dad, Mum and I went to the hospital and sat opposite the admitting psychiatrist and Dad asked 'What is wrong with my son' but Peter was not given a diagnosis. The psychiatrist said that while a child was approaching puberty his emotional state was in flux. 'Any fixed statement about his condition might lead to wrong treatment of symptoms.' When Dad tried to insist that a diagnosis was imperative so he could peruse the best help and treating team, the psychiatrist looked at Peter's file and said 'Peter is an unusual case. He has clear symptoms of Bipolar Mood Disorder but also hears voices and often has full-blown fantasies, which suggests Schizophrenia. Because he is only twelve any labeling is very destructive. Psychiatric problems are always hit and miss and we will all have to proceed with as open a mind as possible. There is no quick fix.' My Dad looked at this highly educated man without comprehension 'What, do you mean? Is there no prescription for what to do with my son? He's not the first child to light a fire or attack his sister or an animal. Others cause a public nuisance. You are the doctor, you have studied and you will take my money. Tell me what to do.' The all-knowing psychiatrist said nothing.

Time stopped and I moved automatically about my daily tasks. Got up, had breakfast, went to school, sat through days filled with lessons where I strained to absorb what little I could without being able to read. I watched on while gaggles of giggling girls lived life of promise and returned home each evening to wait for the next frightening foot to fall. My parents were there but absent, consuming each waking hour with meaningless jabber, arguments or fights about what would come next. We were now drawn together, a small impotent team of ghosts floating uncertain and petrified on the edge of existence. At night, the Boogieman hid behind every closed door and in every dark corner. He was larger than life and I could hardly breathe.

Somehow this tragedy ended when my brother came home and life was normal for a while. Peter settled after ECT, took his medication and got well enough to attend school. He studied, slept, ate and sometimes even smiled. I didn't let go of my apprehension but almost began to believe I might survive, live and share my life with others and then, a crushing episode.

This recollection, hard wired into my memory, still fuels my nightmares as I smell his stale breath, feel his fleeting touch and hear the lascivious voice of the suspended shapeless Boogieman.

Within four months Peter was high again, but this time Dad had thoroughly searched the mental health system and found a private sanitarium, which claimed success with schizophrenia. I went with Mum, and Dad to have Peter committed into this private mental hospital. The main buildings were set well back from the road behind a high brick wall. The grounds had well-manicured lawns bracketed by colorful flowerbeds. The central structure was clean and welcoming but as we approach the entrance, I noticed that all the windows were high up, small and heavily barred. We had to ring a bell and were ushered into the building through a substantial wooden door. A burly guard dressed in a crisp clean uniform had a baton hanging from his waist.

Peter wouldn't walk into the locked ward so we led the way. An open courtyard with shiny polished concrete floor was open to the sky. A couple of benches were fixed to the ground. Several men gaped at us as we entered. Peter looked around, dashed for a drainpipe and up the six-metre wall. Before we know it, he was waving to us from the roof. Then he was gone.

Mum, Dad and the attendant rushed out and the door swung shut. I was trapped, locked in with these drooling maniacs with hanging jaws and glazed grinning eyes. One stood directly in front of me dribbling. He leered 'I'm your dentist and I'm going to drill ye. Come here cunt.' I froze, fear so intense that my heart would burst.

I remembered the smell of the dentist's stale breath on my cheek, my bile rising and his lunatic laugh. He grabbed at me and plundered, poked and prodded. I pushed him away turned on him and hurled my lungs out. I was turning myself inside out. My skin wouldn't hold the churning fluids in. Everything was exposed and only when I was empty could I stop. My whole being was greasy, sticky and so stinky.

He reached out for me again. I shoved him aside, hammered on the door and howled. When it opened, I ran. I hurtled headlong down the manicured driveway into the street and out towards town. I ran for my life not thinking, not stopping until I crossed a main road I knew. Philip my steadfast friend lived just down from the intersection. I turned and ran a couple more blocks fighting for breath. Then I lifted my head, straightened my clothes and continued my search. I finally found Philip's place a sobbing wreck, not able to speak. I remember his arms around me, and his soothing voice. He comforted me, sent me off to bathe, gave me a mug of steaming Milo, put me to bed and sat by my side until I fell into a fitful sleep. He came to me when I screamed and woke me before I could dream.

The next morning when I woke Philip asked what happened. My head ached, felt as if it would split apart if I spoke so I turned away. Philip sat quietly by my side and rubbed my forehead. 'Is that any better?' I tried to smile and asked for some water. He brought it and I drank. Then slowly I pieced together what had happened. Locked in, I was assaulted by several men. The dentist had grabbed me, pulled my skirt up, and tried to penetrate me but I had kicked and screamed while he grasped at me with one hand and rubbed his grotesque red penis with the other. An acrid white substance had seeped out around his fingers. A fingernail of the grasping hand had drawn blood. At first there were blank stares and then two others began to scratch, prod and poke. When I did not keep still enough someone bit my arm and wrenched it behind my back. This arm was still immensely painful. He was about to penetrate me when I wet myself and began to retch again causing all the inmates to stop and stare. I got to my feet kicked wildly, ran to the door and hammered until someone came.

As Philip listens, I sobbed 'I'm dirty. I'll never be clean.' For ages, I could think of nothing else. I wanted to scratch my skin off but Philip held my hands and told me I was beautiful, clean, and immensely brave. When I was done talking, Philip held me again as I fell asleep. When I woke he asked if he could contact my parents but I sobbed again, this time uncontrollably 'You can try but they won't be there. They only care about Peter and he's gone.' Philip phoned my parents home but there was no answer.

I don't know what happened in the two days that passed before my parents came to pick me up. But when Philip opened the door, my father's black hair had gone grey.

***

I loathed Peter's insistent bewildering illness and hated that my parents didn't notice me. I waited each day to be included while Mum tore her hair, drank, sobbed and yelled about her lost life. 'My beautiful son!!! You've stolen my beautiful son. God damn you. Let me die. I can't go on. My son, my son.' Now drink became her analgesic. She soaked herself stupid and stared into space. Our beautiful cosy lounge became a mausoleum, my brother's sanity the coffin within. I tried to reach Mum. To touch her outstretched arm and clenched fist as she punched the air but she pushed me aside. ' You don't understand. Go away, leave me to die.' My father was at work or with Peter. Who knows where but his grief was palpably present. The only time we connected was in our misery as we climb into the car for the excruciating visits to the safely locked ward where Peter lay comatose in a strangling suffocating catatonia. I wasn't allowed to stay away so when we went to the well-kept sanatorium I hung on to Dad's sleeve helplessly until we left. Each of these days was a never-ending hell. Alone in my room each night the day's alienation was replaced by a deeply disturbed sleep. Silent and sobbing I awaited the same petrifying nightmare.

I crouched in a corner listening for danger, sniffed the damp air and struggled to control my uneven breathing. It was imperative that I stilled my heart and readied myself to flee. I was transfixed and terrified. A huge amorphous apparition crept across the ground and its shadow finally fell across my body. This strange consuming company now ready to pounce.

Heart, hammering in my chest. Air sucked from my body. I summoned all my strength to duck away and under the approaching menace, but found myself trapped against a soaring wall. No exit. Cornered my heart felt as if it would burst . . . and then with all of the breath squeezed out of my lungs I would shake free of this limp cringing heap. My spirit would leave my body and I was free to flee or to watch.

Just as well because the Boogieman was back.

Music and Mayhem

I sat cross-legged on the rug in the lounge and worked at learning. I was never going to read but I had watched Peter lose and regain whole slabs of knowledge and today I was determined to find enough courage to shape my own learning. In Geography, our teacher had suggested using a simple template to ensure we covered everything we needed when we wrote about a country. 'Draw the map and then use my mnemonic PRCPCCD. P for position, R is relief and drainage C climate, P population, C cities and towns, C communications and finally D development.'

I traced a map of Africa, shaded the mountains and valleys and then meticulously copied each main city in South Africa to the map with my finger under each name to prevent spelling errors. Laborious. I let my focus shift, heard guitar music coming from Peter's room. Beautiful, a Spanish tune in a minor key, every note crystal clear. This music like fine-spun velvet soft, gentle, simple and full of harmony. Today Peter was OK. I sighed. Hard to believe he was calm again.

***

Peter was always consumed by music.

Shut away in his airplane Peter would hum or listen to music. Whether he listened, played or created, the music was my thermometer always. Told me what was happening inside.

Often Pete and Zorbas our big tabby cat would snuggle together in front of the radiogram and listen, Zorbas at Peter's side purring and beating his tale against the carpet in time to the music. Pete conducted and sometimes sang. He loved music, mainly Mozart like Mum. Gave it his all, face etched with concentration as he followed and hummed theme and harmony, smiled and swayed, played the same piece over and over followed each resonating strand.

Jealous of my baby brother until the mountain accident - why? Without him, junior school would have been unbearable. He protected me. When he withdrew he still showed his feelings as he hummed, or hissed or grumbled with tempo and tune. He never resiled from expressing his irrepressible deep emotions.

Once when a fight was followed by a hostile silence followed. Dad slammed out of his office and Mum stormed off to her room. Peter came to the lounge where I huddled on the couch knees under my chin, scared to go through my parent's room to my own. He looked at me, said nothing, went to the record cabinet took out Prokofiev's Peter and the wolf and played it loudly. He sat still and listened until the place where the wolf stalks Peter. At this point, he jumped to his feet and marched up and down arms swing wildly. When the crescendo finished, he lifted the needle, set it down again at the beginning of this passage, and marched again. Five or six times he played it through as his marching intensified. Finally, he played it through hands at his side and then listened as the music continued and the piece lightened with the entry of the bird. He listened intently, head cocked to one side, came and touched my hand, turned off the music and went to his room. I curled up on the couch, drew Zorbas close and closed my eyes. Peter's agitation was spent as was mine.

My 'Comma Prima' performance excited Peter. He wanted it perfect. I had a recording to practice at home. For several days I sang trying to get the words just right and to follow tempo and nuance of the singer's voice. 'Jill you are not an opera singer you need to sing it your way.' We rehearsed for days. Sometimes Peter demonstrated a sad rendition and on others happy. He paced my singing, said 'Don't sing through your nose.' As I followed and watched Peter conduct according to his mood. Sometimes fast and almost staccato and on others, gentle and lilting. By the time he finished my singing was polished, I was confident and Peter was simply ecstatic.

At high school, I was told that every young lady should play a musical instrument. Mum insisted on piano because I could learn and practice at school and the fees covered classes and practice. While I had a good voice could harmonize, I had no talent for piano, failed hopelessly and another simpler instrument was suggested. I was also pretty hopeless with the guitar.

It lay around the house. Peter picked it up and was soon playing simple tunes. Mum enchanted suggested some lessons. He began once a week but did so well that his teacher suggested he play more seriously. Peter was delighted and spent many hours alone with my guitar learning the compositions of others and creating his own. He played solo or as accompaniment to our singing.

Guitar became almost an obsession as Peter made it resonate with his extravagant range of moods. When depressed, his guitar dripped with sadness, his melancholy so deep and pervasive sounding, it might weep at his desolation. I remember sitting knees against my chest gulping back tears of distress at my brother's never-ending hollowness. The sweet despair clung to my soul.

On another occasion, Peter's music was extremely hyped as he headed towards a bipolar high after his first hospitalization. On a spring evening towards the end of my second year of high school; I sat outside, long phone line dragged onto the verandah beyond my parent's earshot, chatting with Anneke. Peter followed plucking at his guitar. I asked him to leave but Annie intervened 'His playing is great I am enjoying it' so I say 'OK stay.'

At first Peter sat, his strumming gentle then he came closer to the phone and moved his hands more rapidly. I stopped listing to Annie and focused on his staccato beat. Peter was now hitting the strings and body of the guitar faster and faster. My heart started pounding and I watched as Pete jumped to his feet and wove back and forwards like a trapped animal unable to rest, up and down, up and down. His restlessness contagious I got up and began to shift from foot to foot in an uncomfortable, breathtaking shuffle. My heart beat unevenly in response to the agitated percussion. Annie called my attention back to the phone and said she was getting uptight because of Peter's playing and she wanted to go.

Within a month of this incident and after a couple more restless, raw, jamming sessions Peter set his school clothes alight and I saw his music as harbinger of the oncoming storm. I began to predict the crescendos before life fell apart and his music slowed and became melancholy. I expected the intolerable abyss of lows, swallowing all joy, and awaited the descent into places so deep that Peter was beyond reach.

The most exhilarating and exhausting music came as Peter skyrocketed out of depression and into the euphoria of a bipolar high. The guitar trembled with ecstasy. It would writhe and swell, alive with the rhythm of his body, and thunder and sizzle as the resonance filled the air with an electric expectation before the final climax and explosion into action so intense that it was no longer within control. Now I knew that hospitalization was inevitable because Peter had moved beyond containment.

I remember Peter, a dark writhing silhouette against the blue sky at the apex of our roof, thrashing out a rebellious Spanish solo on his guitar to the thunderous applause of the neighborhood servants. They loved his extravagant 'chutzpah.'

***

Peter is on the roof, this time removing the gutters to install a hydroelectric system. Dad had said electricity and water bills were sky high and Peter was rigging up a system to recycle water and generate electric current to reduce household expenditure. Well ahead of his time our Peter, and removing the front door - can't remember why.

On a beautiful spring afternoon I lay out on the verandah well-oiled, face turned to the sun, working on my summer tan when a massive truck backed up. A deliveryman said 'Hi. Got a delivery' and started unloading enough equipment to fill a factory, stainless steel tool bench, stand up jigsaw, sander. Well who knows really? 'Sign here. Good stuff but not cheap.' I signed acknowledging only that the goods were delivered. No more. Who was I, an angry rebellious teenager to argue?

Peter thrilled began throwing out tired old garden tools to make way for what was definitely not fitting through the door or finding space inside our shabby old shed. He spoke joyously as he worked. 'Now I can really change the roofline and recycle the excess storm water. Now the pump . . .'

Used to the bizarre and protective of myself I said nothing and waited for the inevitable furore when Dad got home.

Dad arrived 'What the hell is going on? Why isn't it in the shed? Peter responds from inside the shed '...because I have got some new tools to fix the roof.'

'The roof's just fine.'

'Yes but the water bill is high and electricity is expensive and. . .
'

'For God's sake Peter!'

Peter stomped off angry. When a furious Dad phoned the company to demand explanation of why they sold equipment to a twelve year old on credit, they claimed my signature was an acceptance of responsibility for the purchase. Dad countered 'A competent businessman checks the credit status of any customer before delivery.' This worked. The equipment, only slightly soiled, was removed the next day.

Another confrontation, today a cold June holiday, Peter was 'normal', his music gentle and his speaking tone mellow, a warm, loving and peaceful youth. Everyone including Tom, Louisa and the cat responded by allowing themselves closer when this occurred. Today Peter and Zorbas were cuddled in front of the fire, Peter playing guitar and Zorbas, now old, stretched to his full length in front of the hearth. Come evening Zorbas wandered into the kitchen, wolfed his meal, and returned to the lounge, brushed against Peter's leg, purred and returned to his cozy spot in front of the fire. Unfortunately Zorbas had eaten to quickly and soon stood bent over his front legs and disgorged his undigested meal onto the Persian rug just as Dad walked in. I rushed for a cloth and began to clean.

As Dad instructed me in the finer details of cleaning, Zorbas was sick again. Dad grabbed the scruff of his neck and drop kicked him out the back door. Peter incensed, grabbed Dad by the backside and kicked him using the same refined skills Dad had demonstrated. I laughed, gagged, and kept on cleaning. Dad humphed at Peter, who picked himself up and went to his room.

And so images push through the fog of my forgetting. Some hilarious, some sad, some accurate and some embellished with time.

One I remember without context. Peter was offered a scholarship to go to Segovia in Spain to study guitar but my parents decided he was not stable enough to pursue this dream. Peter's playing impressed others as much as his family.

***

In my last three years of senior school, Peter was often hospitalised and each time we hoped this might be the last episode. At times, my schooling was severely affected and I turned more often to Anneke, also with much to carry. Her Mum was batty and her Dad had another woman, leaving her, two sisters and an older brother to look after Mum. 'I'm sick to death coping. Peter sounds worse though.'

'He's getting madder as the days pass. My parents will probably split soon and leave me drowning in his madness.' We recognized in each other a fellowship and our friendship grew. Now I trusted another with my fears. The Boogieman retreated a little.

***

Mum and I were summoned to the head mistress because my behavior was disruptive. 'Jill is deceitful; she accused your son of tearing up her homework. She is also not bright. Perhaps she'll make a good housewife. It's now time for her to join the non-academic stream and focus on her social skills. She relates poorly to the other girls.' I gritted my teeth and swore I'd achieve a higher academic qualification than her before I quit study.

Towards the end of high school, the dynamics in our family shifted a little. With Peter ill so often it was difficult to live a normal family life, and as he slipped further and further away Mum began sharing her shattered dreams.

Boys, boys, boys

I remember sitting with Mum in her bedroom at about seven o'clock as she dressed for a mountain club dance. She sat in front of her large dressing table donning earrings. In a long peacock blue dress she was utterly gorgeous and I cried. 'I'll never be beautiful like you.'

I saw myself as plain, which suited me fine after the incident in the mental hospital. Being either shapely or attractive was bound to bring trouble and I hated being touched anyway. Later I became ambivalent, scared of attracting any attention or closeness of any kind was horrifying, but as a normal growing girl I also had dreams.

I'd fantasise about meeting a guy who found me beautiful and together we would ride away into the sunset. As I dreamed I hummed a consistent theme 'and you'll look sweet upon the seat of a bicycle built for two.' With this dream I could face the realities of my life.

***

Fear was a constant companion and managing it became my unconscious preoccupation. Resilience was illusive so I tried different strategies. Secreting myself in hedges or my bed worked while I was little. Sheltering under Louisa's bed was a wonderful backstop but only available when she was elsewhere. Hiding silent in the crowd was uncomfortable but as I grew older usually successful. Sleeping failed because of the Boogieman. As I matured, boys or young men who enjoyed the Sir Galahad role were among the most reliable. I sought out such saviours more often.

First was Philip my saviour when my parents forgot me in their chase after Peter escaped from hospital. Then came Sid, not a personal Galahad but a young man who led a school camping trip snowed under by a blizzard in the mountains.

Rob a wonderful young man gave me his all through my last years of high school and the first year of University. I met him while holidaying with the family on old year's eve.

We had camped on a secluded beach away from others. I was angry and alone. Of course I was with family but family is not company. Finally I persuaded my parents to take me to a place with people, and here we were at popular Plettenburg bay. As soon as we arrived I jumped out of the car, left family behind and ran for the beach.

A perfect day! The camel brown beach, a giant sickle moon stretched long and warm beneath an infinite sky, the lapping waves foam-capped, a gentle breeze sighed and 'ahh . . .' the beach was buzzing with beautiful people, my age. When I reached the waves I stopped. How would I make contact with others? My heart sank!

It took just a few minutes and I wasn't alone.

From first sight I was besotted. He was tall, bronzed and beautiful, his eyes a gentle hazel brown. Friendly and considerate he offered a towel alongside his, came swam with me and spoke in a gentle gravelly voice as we soaked in the sun. We walked for miles first on the beach and then on a wild, rocky isthmus and 'Oooh! . . .' he offered me his hand as I jumped a small stream.

That evening he asked me to a beach party. I sat between his knees and listened while his brother sang the old year out and the New Year in. I watched the fire burn bright and smelled the sea. At midnight we kissed in the moonlight beside the gently lapping ocean and I was in love.

My family left for home the following day, and while I wished with all my heart for his call it didn't come for several long weeks. Our first real date was to the cricket. Without the vaguest interest in this or any sport I would have gone anywhere to be with Rob. We spent a whole day holding hands in the sun on the Western stand at the Wanderers Stadium. A boring game, nothing seemed to happen. We got a hot dog and coke for lunch and returned. Our conversation was easy, the sun warm and I felt tingly all over. Was this the beginning of love? It didn't matter that I wasn't interested in the game, being with this hunk was enough. His voice was deep and gravelly, what more could there be?

And then Rob grabbed my hand tightly and pulled me to my feet. A roar went around the grounds. The whole stadium was on its feet. Graeme Pollock had just hit 200 runs against Britain and the crowd were in uproar, stamping their feet and clapping their hands. I clapped too yelling 'Go South Africa' and for the first time in my life I remember being proud of my country. Wow!

Rob walked me home in the cool of the evening. The cloudy sky was an indigo blue reaching for infinity; a gentle breeze played through the trees we walked under and around the shirt tails of a striped blue shirt Rob had offered to protect me from the afternoon sun. We talked about our pride in and pain for South Africa, our beautiful country that had got politics so wrong. We were together and I was happy. He took me to the front door still chatting. A perfect day! Why must it end?

As we stood on the front steps saying a reluctant goodbye mum pushed past us swearing 'Get fucked'. Rob's mouth dropped, his beautiful face went crimson and he retreated down the path. I followed him to the gate saying a very embarrassed goodbye. I was mortified. My wonderful day ruined. I'd not see him again.

It took a while but Rob phoned. I met him away from home and went back to his very posh house not far from my school. We talked for hours about unfortunate families. I told him about Mum, Dad and Peter and he told of his mum who had died leaving his dad with three young children. His dad had married again to a woman with two children, a boy his age and another. He felt out of place like I did. While his family was very couth he was also unhappy. I had found a companion, friend and first real love. With him I felt sane and whole and loveable, my alpha and omega.

Mum took me overseas and I was terrified that I would lose him. I was too grown up to cling, so suggested he date others while I was away. Mum had coached me 'If you hold too tightly you will lose your man.' As we sat sipping lemonade watching his brother play tennis, I talked of maturity and freedom while my insides screamed don't go, don't let this gem out of your sight, but he was too important to cling to so I bravely suggested who and where. 'If our love is real it will survive you dating another.' What high drama.

Overseas with Mum

'So many things have happened to your Mum.' Dad sat me down and began 'She's had a few very difficult years and we have agreed together that a trip to Europe would help get these traumas into perspective. Remember the accident in Kransburg. After that we went through a particularly bad patch and then came Sharpeville and all her old fears of Hitler and of course Peter. It has been excruciating for her.'

Dad and Mum had been having counselling and the counsellor had suggested that mum needed to integrate all the things that had happened. To begin she should go back to Germany and see that her home had survived the Holocaust. Dad needed to stay and watch out for Peter so the task fell to me to go as Mum's companion. 'Guide and help Mum put things in perspective.'

All very well but what about me in this exercise. I'd also been through a bit but was now getting on quite well. I finally had a super relationship with a gorgeous guy and was doing better at school. I wanted nothing more than to live, work hard and learn more about loving from my gorgeous guy. Truth be known I was terrified that, if I left him for a moment, another would jump in and my life would be ruined forever. But how could I say no to a trip to Europe. Impossible.

***

Tired and disoriented, the walls closed in. A tunnel of buildings below a smudged grey sky stretched to infinity. The air dripped with a cloying stifling heat and as I walked, the dense air pushed back against my swollen legs. My eardrums hammered, reverberating with over-animated voices in an irksome lilting language, meaningless to me. Who needs twelve hours in the air and why wouldn't Mum just let me sleep? Why this strange city with no sign of foliage, just old crumbling walls, a decaying antiquity. Nothing contemporary or familiar, I wanted to escape. Go home. Now!

'Jill we are in Europe the world I came from, because I want you to know and understand my warp and weft, the fabric of me; to connect you with my past. This trip is a gift. We start in Rome because fascism began here.'

Irate and indifferent, I swallowed my desire to run from all she stood for and wanted to show me. Rome was just too foreign.

For three endless days, I dragged behind her; the Trevi Fountain, Colosseum, Vatican City were all better in the glossy prints. Then in the Sistine Chapel we lay on our backs and looked up at the ceiling and I was transfixed. Dad and Mum had often spoken about the art and architecture of Europe and its profound and complex impact on the people who lived and breathed antiquity, but here I was a small insignificant creature at the centre of an overpowering expression of God's universe. I was invited to look into the heavens, as if God had created a pathway to understanding his awe-inspiring greatness, but it was painted by men. 'Wow!'

I began listening to things Mum said. Perhaps it was worth getting to know her world. She talked about how she had taken the antiquity of Europe for granted until she left. She had hated the weight of history she carried merely by living with it. How delighted she'd been at the openness and light of Africa and how this had turned to profound homesickness as she realized European history built stone on stone made her who she was. The weight of this world had shaped her understanding of life. 'Without it I'm nothing. Europe shaped my history and I see the openness and naïveté of Africa through this lens.'

It was 1965, spring and Europe began to blossom. I turned to the sun and opened myself to this experience. Nothing too terrible so far and Mum was happy. With Rome done, we got into our magnificent little Fiat Topolino and motored up the West coast of Italy, through France and into Germany.

We camped again in Munich, setting our tent in a wonderful green field just outside the old town and headed off to explore. The air was silky soft, the countryside filled with buttercups. Campers eager to connect but respectful and, most important, the toilet block was pristine. In Rome things were more lackadaisical and a little less sanitary. We spent the day walking the old streets. We sat in a café and listened to the singsong southern accent. This one I understand, the language not dissimilar to the one I heard over breakfast when Dad and Mum reminisced about the old days before they left. I asked Mum about the times she camped in Germany.

'You were for us or against us. As comrades we did many things together. We were anti-bourgeois, saw religion as the opium of the masses and resisted authority, but were fiercely loyal to our Jewish heritage. We had to be in the face of Fascism. Wild and passionate, we loved life. All was important, art, music, architecture, culture but we were interested in the future, in communalism, and Communism, not in stuffy ideas of the past. For Europe to flourish we needed innovation and inspiration for our floundering world. We climbed, walked, sang and camped but most important we learned together. In the Kameraden life had much sweetness despite the coming storm.'

I asked Mum about her Kameraden friends and was surprised to hear several names I knew well. They had followed Dad's South African relocation and were part of a transplant of strongly connected Jewish youth, who had forsaken religion, rallied against anti-German prejudice and believed that enlightened communism may offer an alternative inclusive politic accessible to all.

Mum was relaxed and I enjoyed her company; surprising, as I hadn't often experienced such gentleness or rapport. Never before had I entered her inner world and was fascinated that her constant nagging attacks on Fascism were grounded in a coherent philosophy, shared with others.

We whiled away the afternoon, went to the Hofbrau House for a beer and 'wurst', sat in a full eating hall at a long refectory table with perhaps ten other carousing beer drinkers, ate and sang drinking songs. Mum told a young man about Africa, the new but most ancient of worlds and I chatted with another who spoke beautiful English about 'The Beatles'. It was wonderful to be part of something I know from the inside. The tunes we sang come from my heart despite not having sung them before.

We left a little tipsy, arm in arm like sisters or perhaps friends, singing as we tramped back to our car. Then suddenly Mum stopped, shaking. 'What is it Mum?'

'The Gestapo, those boots.' She ran headlong for the car and had the engine well and truly going by the time I get in. She spoke in German. 'Hurry we must get away. Now.' The engine shrieked as we pulled away as quickly as a small Topilino could go. In camp, Mum sat in the car, stared ahead and said nothing.

I could not move her. Later she came, crawled into the tent and sleeping bag. I asked what she was afraid of but she could not speak. I stroked her arm and she shrugged me away. I asked about fear again and she answered but in German 'I will stay in my clothes. Be ready to run.'

'Yes Mum! Try and sleep.'

When I woke the next morning Mum was up and the camp stove was going. 'How did you sleep?'

'I didn't.' I asked again 'What are you afraid of' now scared that I would not be able to care for her myself. What the hell was going on? Who could I contact if she flipped into anger. Vigilant I kept prodding but Mum could not verbalize her fear. 'Let's go see what we have come to see.' Mum became grumpy and biting and I fought to stay present. No wonder I became a shrink, I certainly had the training.

A day or two later Mum relaxed and told me that it had been Gestapo in boots that had come for the Jews. She had seen storm troopers smash windows and break up gatherings. She left Germany before people were forcibly removed but she had seen many films emphasizing boots to encapsulate the horror of forced removal of Jews to the camps. These boots were her symbol of the Holocaust horror.

We visited her old teacher Frau Professor Doctor Fucker. What a name, I couldn't believe it. She was frail, white haired but upright, well groomed and as sharp as a new pin. Her eyes twinkled as she held the door for us. We entered her traditional meticulously appointed apartment. It looked across the Rhine towards Frankfurt's magnificent Gothic cathedral. We sat down to tea served in lovely Hutschenreuther china and begin to talk. 'I was so ashamed of my countrymen and saddened at losing touch with people like your mother. I feared for her life. How wonderful to see her alive and vibrant. Your striking blue eyes still sparkle Else, and that hair that will not lie down.' She turned to me. 'Is she as brazen with you as she was with me? Your mother was alive, up to something, what a temper and her wonderful intelligence, such a pity she could not fulfill her dream and be a doctor.' I smiled. I wanted to say that the temper was now a full-blown fury, difficult to control and bloody scary; that managing Mum and myself exhausted me and was more than anyone could expect. I wanted to tell her about Peter, Dad, and the horror of South African politics but instead I asked for another piece of Sacher torte and kept my own counsel.

On a clear sunny morning a couple of days later, Mum woke me. 'Today I will show you why I brought you to Germany. I have seen this before when I visited and perhaps you have seen on film but now I will show you history. A symbol of what Hitler did.' We went to a small town nearby, crossed a cobbled square and rounded a corner. Ahead of us was a small Romanesque church. Mum put her hand on my arm and without words directed me to stop and look.

A high stock brick wall had a board affixed. Across the top was written in German, English and French. 'The names below are of people still missing. If you know of their whereabouts please report within.' Rows and rows of names appeared beneath these words; perhaps five hundred in all. Red ticks next to the name of a few indicated that this person had been found; many names were crossed through in black signifying that a death had been confirmed. The fate of most was still unknown twenty years after the end of World War Two.

Mum turned to me 'You've asked why I can't move on. I have seen raised eyebrows when I hark back to Hitler and I know you think 'get over it' but there's a similar list in every village and town in Germany. This is what Hitler did to Jews and nothing can be forgiven until the whereabouts of these people are confirmed. Every person deserves to know what has happened to family and friends.' She covered her face, sobbed and I stood silent until her hands drop to her side. She looked at me. 'I'm sorry Mum.'

I wonder whether the boards are there still. It is so easy to forget.

***

About a week after this lesson, we woke to a glorious sunny morning. Camped beside the Rhine the previous night, we had celebrated the delights of a beautiful Nacktkarsch mosel, eaten, sung and chatted with other campers around a campfire. I looked out through the tent flaps across the wide river at a magnificent castle perched atop a rock wall that rose straight out of the Rhine. Pulling my yesterday's shorts out of my rucksack I looked up. Mum said 'I had a premonition, phoned home and Peter is ill again.' Peter had been hospitalized the night before. 'Dad said we should not come but I cannot drive through Europe and ignore my tragedy.' That was it, I knew Mum. No point arguing. Angry that my needs were again ignored I swallowed my disappointments about missing Britain and began to pack.

Mum phoned the airport and changed our flights but could not get immediate flights so we lost only a week. We rejigged our onward journey, which included Britain, but cut our French sojourn short. Both France and Britain were fun but enjoyment was diminished, Mum preoccupied and me jealous. Peter had usurped me again from six thousand kilometers away. Blast him.

We left for Johannesburg - my special time with Mum sullied, my holiday cut short.

First thing I did on return was call Rob. We met and he told me about the wonderful evening he had spent with Sue. My heart sank I had lost him. But then he smiled and asked me about my experiences and all was forgotten in his wonderful gaze.

This man was all I had dreamed of. We became inseparable. He helped with my schoolwork. He was a year ahead in school and often coached me. I had a good memory and with his help found ways of circumventing reading. He believed I was smart and seemed to love discussing my work. He said it helped him consolidate his learning. He encouraged me to make the most of opportunities my good teachers offered and talked endlessly about University should I continue studying after school.

We toiled to make South Africa a more equitable and democratic country as we dreamed of building our future together, met with other young people to talk about what a true democracy looked like. Would we vote for a qualified franchise built on education because people needed to understand government to vote or would we support a party who believed in one man, one vote? Ideas clarified we joined the Progressive Party's Young Progs and worked to support the work of Helen Suzman in her electorate. We distributed written information, canvassed from house to house and shared our ideas with others. When Helen was re-elected to parliament we celebrated and dedicated ourselves to working harder. Politics would always be part of our lives.

We window-shopped for furniture and spoke of the children we would have together. Talked endlessly about building a safe, equitable future.   Rob spoke with Peter and played chess with my father. Mum loved him and Rob became used to her outspoken ways. We camped together in the mountains and Rob learned to love the outdoors.

But then Peter got ill again and my fear grew and alas in my mind Rob was not big or strong enough to keep Peter at bay and fight my demons. He was after all only six foot tall and my fears were enormous. I began to seek a bigger and braver man.

Look - a life of my own

I sat by our garden gate in my lucky blue shorts, hopeful but terrified. Today of all days I needed to intercept the post and get to my matriculation results first. Peter, Mum and Dad agreed with my headmistress' prognostications that I would do badly. After all, I was functionally illiterate. Dad had been saying for a week that the only career worth pursuing was to become a plumber because each time a drain blocked our budget was blown for a couple of months. 'You can't read or spell so I'm serious, it's shitty work but the pay is good. You'll never get into university.'

I had put in a superhuman effort in the run up to my final exams. Taken by my geography teacher's belief that anyone could win if they worked hard enough. This pedantic lady with her beehive hairstyle and penchant for extravagant usually bright floral dresses was my saviour. She conscientiously taught us how to commit information to memory.

'Summarize. Print these two lines to a book row. Use mnemonics to remember what is important. I have given you the PRCPCCD example in geography copy this idea in other subjects.' I followed these principles to the letter painstakingly reduced all the important stuff I had underlined in textbooks. For each subject I chose one or perhaps two questions I would tackle and wrote trial essays using short sentences and simple words. Where possible I got the teacher to tell me what was missing. Then I refined these until each was in point form and took no more then one page. I prepared mnemonics, which I wrote boldly across the top, gave each letter a paragraph and used coloured pens to write and underline paragraph subtitle I needed to remember. This created a pattern I could visualise and I was able to memorize enough to have at least one topic I could cover in any section of each exam I sat. I worked by day and into every night of the study break. By the time the exams came, I knew each essay off pat and was confident that I would be able to understand any question well enough to shape my answers. Only when the exams were over did I allow myself the luxury of returning to self-doubt. Waiting for my results was excruciating.

When the postman finally came, my hands shook and I couldn't open the letter. I forced myself to breath, tore the envelope, looked at my marks and burst into tears. My study had worked. I got a second-class Matriculation exemption. I had achieved good enough scores to gain a place at the Witwatersrand University to study for a BA. I sat in the path tears streaming down my face. Finally, I had made it. I had something no one could take away.

When mum walked in from work about an hour later, she saw me and sighed. 'Well it's not that bad Jill. I am sure you will find something.'

'But I passed.'

'You what? But your headmistress said you'd not make it.'

I held up my results. 'Wow!'

I got no more from Mum but Rob was elated. 'I knew you could do it!'

That evening over dinner, there were no congratulations. Instead, Mum who had seemed pleased for me that afternoon now celebrated her successful contribution to my school fees, Peter spoke about how he managed to keep up despite his illness and attendance at a public school and Dad said 'Don't expect me to pay for your study.'

I was mortified and slammed out saying 'Don't worry I won't.'

I rushed to my room and phoned Rob. 'No one even said well done. I hate them. They don't care one bit.'

'Well I do' he reminded me. 'Now remember we talked about the possibility of you training as a teacher.' The next day I went off to the teacher's training collage and asked for a studentship. When I told Dad he was impressed with my taking initiative. I indentured myself for three years after university and a week later was doing my first round as a student teacher. I was soon convinced that I couldn't spend all day every day in front of a class full of high school students. However, I was hell bent on proving I needed no financial support so stuck it out knowing that after the initial placement there was a full six months before I had to go into a classroom again. For now it was enough to know that my parents would not pay for university. I would stay at home and work during holidays for pocket money and I would think of some way out of my contract by the end of Semester 1.

***

Peter still suffered recurring bouts of psychosis and manic depression and while doctors were reluctant to label him they pointed Dad towards books. Dad now talked about different possibilities. 'The doctors never commit themselves but the books say that many people with Peter's symptoms suffer with episodes of illness until their late teens. Others only recover at about twenty five or some suffer into their forties. Only a few people remain ill for their whole lives.' When Peter heard this prognosis, he was philosophical. 'I have always been a bit off centre haven't I Dad and it's not all bad. I love the highs. When I have them I am on top of the world.'

He seemed to understand his condition well. ' If I take my medication I can keep up at school. I came first in most subjects this year. I know people avoid contact because they are scared of me but that's OK. I have my books and my guitar for company.'

Peter never seemed aware of the effect of his illness on us. Strange as he was so sensitive to my parents' worries about money and politics. Peter's piercing gaze told me he knew my fear when he chased me hell-bent on destruction but he never spoke about it. He never thought about the expense of his care nor the impact of his behavior on us.

I hoped that someone might see and believe my distress but no one did. When Peter tore up my homework and Mum was called in to see the head mistress she didn't defend me despite having seen Peter tear up my book. When I talked about Peter's illness when we were asked to talk about disability within our community no one heard my distress. By the time I left high school, I had gone past hoping that either Peter or anyone else would ask me what I felt about living with his madness. I found it unbearable. Where I had once had an ally in Peter, I was now adrift in a family where no-one could be trusted emotionally. Everyone flew into uncontrolled unpredictable tantrums. Mum shouted and hit, Dad stormed off and Peter created mayhem. Then calmness would descend. That was life and now that I

77

began to look to a future where I might break away from family I began to hope.

***

I had a deep longing to study psychology at university believing that it may help me understand Peter's illness but was afraid. This fear gripped my gut tearing my inside and I couldn't explain or still this, so I chose subjects I could teach; English, Afrikaans, Geography and Art History.

To my very great surprise, I was one among several students in first year English who struggled to read and I join a special class. Here a group of postgraduate students researching dyslexia and suggested we crawl to open neural pathways. Apparently, people who did not crawl as babies were more likely to have reading difficulties. Crawling requires cooperation between left and right hemispheres of the brain, a key component of reading.

I went home, dumped my bag, went out onto a small sun filled lawn, got down on my hands and knees, and began to crawl. At first I found it was difficult moving first my left arm with my right leg and then right arm and left leg. My right leg and arm moved together followed by my left arm and leg. I slowed down and tried again. This time I lost my balance and fell over. I lay on my back gritting my teeth. Why could I not follow such simple instructions? After a while, I tried again and again until I finally got it. I had never crawled as a baby and here I was getting it right. I spent all of an hour practicing backwards and forwards only stopping when Mum got home and asked what the hell I was doing. I explained and she laughed. The next week we were told to roll a ball backwards and forwards to another, again over and over to open neural pathways. This time I asked Rob for help. We spent the afternoon giggling and rolling a tennis ball backwards and forwards. Despite following these exercises there was no change, I still could not read.

I struggled a while and then to my immense astonishment and enormous relief I began to see words rather than a jumble of letters swimming on a page. Most importantly, having strung the words together, I could actually make sense of what they told me. Finally, I could understand whole chapters and then books. Now I had a chance of getting a degree.

78

***

Dad dropped me at university each morning on his way to work. This gave us almost an hour together five days a week, a larger and more consistent chunk of time then ever before. We talked about Germany before the war. This time I began by saying 'You met Mum in the Kameraden.'

'Yes I was group leader and responsible for her safety. She was the same then as now, always wild and egocentric. She needed taming, discipline.'

'If she was so off the wall why did you get together?'

'I found her intriguing . . . and well she was never out of my mind for long because I had to keep tabs on her.'

'But she came to South Africa. How come?'

'She came on the boat with the others and then we lived in the same flat in Cape Town.'

'But you married her?'

'Marriage has nothing to do with love, it is simply a business contract. I married her only when I went into the air force so she could get a widow's pension if I was killed. I had no intention of spending my life with her.'

I wondered if Dad had said this directly to Mum. They had often sniped and talked about each other and I had certainly used this to play one off against the other but I had not thought through the implications before. 'So you never loved her?'

'I never thought about love, only my commitment to keeping Else and others safe. I had promised Else's father and honoured this.' He was silent a while and then continued. 'One day I may expect the same from you. You may need to make a priority of looking after your brother if he doesn't get better and I am no longer able.'

I was now speechless. Dad's comment about Mum explained the antagonism I had so often seen between them and the affairs I knew they both indulged in, but the implications for me personally were more pressing. I had dreamed of falling in love and then Rob came along, the answer to my dreams. But just recently I had noticed myself scanning the new scene at varsity.

79

Was there perhaps more to life then marrying the first guy to sweep me off my feet? I would keep my eyes peeled but one thing was for sure I needed to love him and him me. I would not spend my life looking after someone and them blaming him for my unhappiness. As for committing myself to being my brother's carer, how could I do this when I constantly needed to save myself from him?

'Dad you don't know what you are suggesting. How can I care for Peter. When he is ill it is all I can do to keep out of his way.'

Dad was silent but he looked at me with a look I remember fifty years later.

We talked about the news. The press was full of reports on South Africa's reputation overseas. The Anti-Apartheid Movement in Britain campaigned for the total isolation of apartheid South Africa, including economic sanctions instead of just consumer boycotts. We were expelled from the Commonwealth. The AAM organized a 'Penny Pledge' campaign, appealing to British people to donate a penny to the movement and sign a pledge to boycott all South African products. The rest of the world came on board and we became increasingly isolated as a country. Boycotts now in full swing were expanded to include sport and culture.

At university I followed student politics with interest. Several people I had known in the Young Progs were active and, while I wasn't involved on campus, I joined the Black Sash, a non-violent white women's resistance organization to protest against the unjust apartheid laws. I'd make good use of the half hour between Dad dropping me at the university gates and my first lecture by standing in line with others, all women, wearing a black sash as a symbol of mourning. We held placards saying 'Reject the 90 Day Detention Bill.'

Dad and I often discussed the dangers of politics and sometimes Dad showed concern about my dogged determination to protest each morning. When I confessed to being thrown into a divisional van alongside my compatriots and taken to police headquarters one morning Dad got angry. 'What the hell are you doing Jill, these bastards mean business. You know people are in detention; that is what's written on your placards. Do you want to become a martyr? Who will that help.'

80

'It's not dangerous Dad. They told us to forget our lefty crap and get on with studying. That's all.'

'All?'

'Well, they took our photos, names and addresses.'

Dad groaned.

'Didn't you and Mum always fight for what you thought was right politically. You took Sam to the border in your boot when they were going to put him under house arrest and what about in Germany?'

We were stopped at the lights. Dad turned away from me and focused for a while on moving forward in the bumper-to-bumper traffic. Then he glanced in my direction and began in a flat resigned voice 'Your mother and I turned from Judaism and committed ourselves to fighting fascism in whatever form it took but we had no choice. Hitler saw to that. Not the luxury afforded you of university. My education came from teachers such as Hanns Katz. He taught us to resist oppression wherever it happened.'

'And Sam? I remember you talking about him.'

'We were life-long friends. I'd do anything for him. We spent many years fighting fascism together. I often visited him in London after his escape. He took up South Africa's fight for freedom from the outside.'

'And you're scared for me?'

'Why else would I tell you these things?'

These discussions were special. I loved Dad listening and responded to me. I felt he was beginning to trust and respect me; that despite his protests to the contrary he liked my standing for justice despite his underlying unease. On the other hand I worried he was beginning to bargain with me that I take on a caring roll in relation to my brother. This was really scary.

***

At university, I learned many things, but most exciting was my connection to family and culture. Annie and I were sitting in an Art history class when several Hanns Katz art works were beamed onto the screen in front of us. I dug her in the ribs.

81

'Remember him, he haunts us. We have one of his paintings on each wall of or sitting room.'

'Of course! Now shut it. I want to hear what they have to say about him.'

The lecturer pointed at the different aspects of a painting. 'Katz was known for his use of light and dark. Glass was either a lens focusing light, promising hope for a future where knowledge, enlightenment and rebirth would flourish' and then pointed at another 'or as an opaque, translucent filter concentrating the angst of the Jewish nation.' He compared these with Katz' lithographs that brutally depicted the desolation wrought by violence, hate and humiliation on a nation and religion by Nazism and validated the trauma, anger and alienation of the death camps.

I turned to Annie again 'My parents were among his closest friends. Dad helped him migrate from Germany and he has a place in history. Wow!'

What I did not tell Annie was that his pastel, the self-portrait of a grey-faced man suffering from cancer was my friend. She knew this work well and loved it, but didn't know that it was him who had heard my countless silent conversations. That he'd kept my counsel and held my secret sorrows.

In Art history I began thinking how my parents had communicated history and place as a deliberate act, immersing Peter and me in art, expressionism, existentialism, music, and their love of the mountains and climbing through camping. Also I began to see Mum and Dad as separate people, separate from each other, from our family and from me.

Mum's ambition to be a doctor had been thwarted so she turned to one of the few choices still open to a young Jewish woman, silversmithing and subsumed herself in the arts. She was now relatively well known in the South African arts scene as eccentric and volatile but also as creative and at the forefront of jewelry design. Her politics were on the extreme edge for South Africa with her outspoken support and articulation of 'one man one vote.' Everyone knew where Mum stood.

Dad while politically involved was more circumspect and conservative. He wanted to teach but without opportunity to study had become a salesman in Germany and was now a successful importer in South Africa. This job was not his life. He loathed it but needed the money to support family, his backroom political endeavors and his passions, supporting young upcoming artists and climbing.

Now it was my turn. Who would I be? How would I move beyond my crippling shyness, my label as the stupid sibling and mediocre no-hoper? How would I move beyond my fear of madness and the stranglehold of Peter's schizophrenia, mania and depression on our family? I'd begun to see glimmers of light. How would I grasp hold of life, create and enjoy my own future. Beginning university had given me hopes and dreams of a wider world. These were mine. Now I needed to live.

***

In each class I attended I made new friends but Annie remained my soul mate. We often met between classes. Today we sat on the Great Hall steps and looked down the main drag, perhaps a hundred metres past grassy lawns filled with students chatting in the mid morning sun, towards the canteen. Annie had just asked me about what Rob and I were doing on the weekend when I looked up, saw the silhouette of a tall slender man with wonderful long legs and turned to her. 'See the guy going into the canteen? He's the man I'm going to marry.'

'What you've been you and Rob forever. Do you even know him?'

'No I don't and things change. I wonder who he is.'

I can't explain what happened that day but my mind was made up. I had to meet Mr. Long legs. I made it my business to find out about him. He was a chemistry student involved in a couple of extra curricular activities, drove a car and worked back stage for the Choral Society. That was all I needed to know. I persuaded Annie to audition with me for the next show. We both got into the chorus and embarked on an all-consuming passion. For three months each year from then on we lived and breathed musical comedy. Rehearsing all weekend and every evening usually followed by raucous parties on Saturdays and Sunday evenings.

David as a backstage Freddy, moved sets, made coffee and played poker during breaks. I learned poker and spent every moment I was not onstage in the pit below playing the game, chatting to the stagehands, flirting with other guys in his presence and inching myself into Dave's consciousness.

He was all I'd been looking for. At six four he was big enough to fight any fear. His politics were foul, and he was obtuse and difficult to understand but I knew instinctively he must be my man. I pursued him mercilessly for several months making sure he was there when I needed a lift, helping clear away after the show, spending time with him and his friends between classes until finally I persuaded him to take an interest.

At first he'd drive Annie and me home from parties. Then he kissed me at my front door as he said goodnight and finally he came home with me to dinner most nights. He was thin and Mum began to foist food on him. 'Who feeds you?'

'I live with other students in Hillbrow and feed myself from my book allowance.' Now Mum was hooked and David became a constant visitor. He argued with Dad, listened intently to our politics, art, and music and sat by as Peter, well at the time, played guitar, began to talk and play chess. Finally I broke off with Rob and David and I became an item. He came away with the family on a two-week holiday and others understood that we were together. It was on this holiday that I told David about Peter's illness and its immense impact on our family. 'That's fine Jill we can manage his madness together if need be.' His unconditional acceptance of Peter, Mum and Dad was very important to me. We became inseparable. David would become a great scientist and I would walk beside him, find a career in my own time and pursue freedom for those less fortunate.

Peter's Triumph

Peter's senior school life was overshadowed by illness. He had shock treatment on numerous occasions, each time his short-term memory would be wiped and he'd lose months of schooling. Despite finding the process demeaning, painful and very dehumanizing Peter would always take it in his stride, come home, take a couple of weeks to settle, relearn what he'd lost, catch up on what he'd missed in the outside world and get on with studying.

First, he'd pick up his guitar and soothe himself, his music a wonderful container for the whole family's anxiety. Sometimes I'd actually bring it to him almost like a headache pills. He'd look angrily at me, take it and begin to play. The anger would thunder through the music, then slow and stop, and he could then put the guitar away and get on with what was next.

Going back to school became routine. Peter had a wonderful sense of the absurd, laughing at himself and his impact on others, helping classmates adjust to his illness. He clowned, exaggerating symptoms and then laughed. This allowed others to laugh with him. After some initial teasing in his first year his situation was discussed in class and his cohort accepted Peter's difference, talked about mental illness and Peter told them what made him special. He also confided in the class that teasing made his life hell and that when he felt bad he tended to dump on others. The teasing stopped. His school accepted Peter's disability, knew his capacity and welcomed him back when ready. They treated him with an almost careless disregard.

Peter now controlled his illness, handled his medication, went with direction about hospital treatment and saw school as a priority He thrived in his last two years of high school keeping well ahead of his age cohort. Our lives became almost routine.

There was one distinct gap in Peter's life. He never had a girlfriend. No one talked about this. It was just too hard.

We believed Peter would proceed to university and find some field to thrive in. His intellect was sharp, why shouldn't he. Peter was quite clearly mad but brilliant. So it came as no surprise that Peter went for and won a scholarship.

My feelings about his success were ambivalent. I admired how he coped with such complex and opposing issues with dignity and yet he was so unpredictable. I never knew whether he would be loving and generous or literally chasing me with me running for my life. I loved and feared Peter.

***

There is a photo of Peter standing alongside three other matriculation students. All had won scholarships to university in a countrywide search for the year's best minds. At the Royal Easter Show Peter had taken David's suggestion and stood at a computer answering a series of questions that increased in difficulty as the one before was answered correctly. Overjoyed we put aside any trepidation about Peter's future when he was among the winners. 'Wow! Peter you are fantastic. The world is your oyster.'

Marriage

David graduated with an honors degree in Chemistry when I was in third year and was offered a job in Pretoria 'It's a good offer Jill. I must go. Working at the CSIR is a great opportunity.'

'OK. It's not far I guess. You can come over on weekends.'

'I'll miss you but we'll chat on the phone during the week and once I'm settled, we can think about you coming over permanently when you've finished your year.'

'What's that mean?'

'Well I'm hoping you will join me as soon as you can. We can live together. You can find a job here and complete the last couple of fill-in subjects to your degree by correspondence. You'd decided that anyway and I'll be doing my Masters.'

'Well I . . .'

'I love you. I'll come over as often as I can. Probably most weekends.' What could I say? I didn't want to live in Pretoria and was disappointed with Dave's lack of romance. I'd hoped he'd get down on one knee and ask me to marry.

'Oh, OK.'

Dave took his very few belongings, rented a flat all of forty-five kilometers away and began work. Hurt, I began to let my thoughts stray. Maybe there was someone else out there. I looked in the mirror, saw a small round face with smoldering hazel eyes surrounded by shiny pitch black hair 'Ah with those eyes, who could resist?' There must be someone more romantic then Dave. 'So flaunt it and see.'

Ah! what fun I had. A coffee, a kiss, a cuddle traded for a lift home. Well why not. 'A cock teaser' they called me. From Monday to Thursday Mum helped me play the come hither game. But then one Friday evening Simon was just leaving as Dave arrived. 'What was that sleaze doing here?' Dave was angry and I became scared. I could not loose my magnificent man. Thirty centimeters taller then me with his long legs, gorgeous scruffy beard, beautiful hazel eyes hidden behind big glasses and a winning smile. Dave was simply my hero, big, strong and protective. He was intelligent, gentle, kind and deliberate. What more could any girl expect of her guy? This man was everything I wanted. Reassured by his distress I gave up the game.

***

Dave asked me to visit him in Pretoria; code for 'was I prepared to be explicit about a sexual relationship?' 'I believe in fidelity, but I want us to make the most of any time we have together and this includes sex.'

It was the sixties but we lived in conservative South Africa and nice girls might sneak off quietly for a bit of nooky but only a wayward young woman would visit a man in his own home alone. 'Nice' girls only left home after a big wedding and until then, they behaved with decorum, which meant no sex before marriage. My parent's example was anything goes, but keep what you do under your hat. I was torn.

Finally, I visited David and stayed over. Shy and feeling exposed as a 'loose' young woman in what I believed was a close knit, gossipy, conservative, church-going community, I wore a curtain ring pretending to be married. It now sits among other memorabilia in my second drawer, a testimony to my naive self-consciousness.

***

Towards the end of David's first year in Pretoria we discussed marriage again but, knowing no one took any notice of us living together, marriage lost its allure.

My dad only married so Mum could get a widow's pension if he died at war and Mum said 'It's over-rated. Only love-struck imbeciles want the white wedding dress and fuss of a wedding day. Marriage costs a fortune, promises everything and delivers disappointment. The big wedding's merely a prelude to being treated like a doormat.'

David's parental lessons weren't much better. Their marriage was sterile and loveless. 'Why don't we just live together? Our commitment isn't dependant on a ceremony. Love will make our lives different.'

I spoke to Dad, sure, that he wouldn't mind but he was adamant 'You are so young Jill, not yet.'

'We are going to be together Dad, you can't stop me!'

'Well if you insist, get married. I lived with Else for eleven years before we married, don't do that. When you fight, a legal commitment is important. It stops you rushing to separation.' Dave ever the sage said. 'I want you with me, let's marry if it's what he wants.'

'I don't want animosity. Perhaps if you ask Dad formally.' David asked Dad for my hand. He in turn asked me if I wanted to marry this all-knowing 'klugscheisser' and when I said yes, he laughed 'Sure.'

We wanted to marry as soon as my exams finished in the magistrate's court with no fuss because neither of us had any religious affiliation. We asked only Dave's parents and my family as witnesses.

My first task was to visit our family doctor. I was reluctant to have children because I was terrified that I might have a mentally ill child like Peter. Dave accepted my concern and suggested we discuss this again once we were settled. 'For now let's have some fun and get used to each other.'

The pill, symbol of the sixties, was only available to married women in South Africa so here I sat across the desk from the family doctor who celebrated my fortune. He looked at me over his half moon glasses and smiled. 'For the first time in history women have control over procreation, you are a lucky young woman. Your experience will be so much easier than women in the past.'

I looked at him stunned. Had he forgotten my mother dragging me into his office five years before because of painful periods and insistence that I be fitted with the Dutch cap because he would not provide a young teen with the pill even for medical reasons? Couldn't he recall my red-faced humiliation as he gave me a lecture on abstinence? 'Young lady you should wait for marriage' or Mum's contemptuous reply 'With the way all young women fuck around, she'll find herself pregnant and I'm not looking after any bastard she has because you won't offer her protection.' Mum's attitude to sex was always that it offered women power over men and that while sex was fun it should never be outside a woman's control. She had cynically used sexuality and good looks to get what she wanted on many occasions. 'Don't make yourself into a doormat by being stupid Jill. Fuck around and have fun by all means but remember kids are a different matter. They hang around your neck forever, so protect and prevent or perish.'

Her earliest sex education had been little different. She forced me to watch our cat giving birth to a litter of kittens. 'You see the blood and how it hurts like hell when she pushes, well that's what comes from fucking around unprotected. You get pregnant, produce bloody babies who mewl and drink you dry. Be warned.' Mum never pulled her punches.

Dave and I decided to travel to Cape Town for our honeymoon and Dave bought a 1947 Volkswagen. We spent several weekends rebuilding the engine. My father, who didn't have a mechanical bone in his body, shook his head '*Meshuggah*'. Don't expect me to rescue you from the middle of nowhere in this ancient German crock and if you fix it on the pavement you will lose all the bits.' He scratched his chin in disbelief when Harold, named after Harold Wilson the British prime minister with the big nose, purred into action. 'Well you have something my boy but you are mad to expect this car to cross the desert.'

While I spoke with disdain of white dresses and veils I wanted to look good and different on my wedding day so spent hours searching through the few specialty shops that sold avant-garde furnishing fabrics. Having made my own clothes all through university I wanted to create something special. I found a wonderful vibrant floral Finnish furnishing fabric and choose a simple loose fitting sheath pattern. Of course being 1969 the dress had to be a mini.

Because our marriage was with only my family and Dave's parents as witnesses, we decided to have a party on the evening after exchanging vows. I invited some of my parents' mountain club friends and as many university mates as I could. Dave did not want anyone from his parents' side. 'There are so many cousins, aunts and uncles I wouldn't know where to stop and my mother is so standoffish. I didn't argue. We told no one about our marriage before the party, as neither Dave nor I wanted a fuss. Mum and I wrote lists, ordered food and booze, and of course, Louisa and Tom did all the preparation.

Mum insisted that as a jeweler she would make my wedding ring. Dave had assumed that he would buy my wedding band but when mum persisted, he backed off. She became obsessed about getting a permit for the gold. Listened to what design I wanted but insisted on artistic license. She sketched and re-sketched the key pattern I asked for. Her design became a symbolic struggle between us as she insisted that the key pattern I wanted in gold on a silver base 'must take the full width of the band' while I didn't want the pattern to reach the edge. The beautiful ring was a constant reminder of her bullying. I now smile. Years later it sits in my lovely jewelry case amongst other beautiful pieces she made and I don't wear. Not a protest, I simply don't like chunky costume jewelry or showy attire and seldom go to places where I am required to dress up.

We married in the Johannesburg Magistrate's Court. David promised to protect, I promised neither to honor nor obey and we both said until death us do part. Knowing about patriarchal relationships, we were both clear we wanted a mutual union. This meant I should think and act for myself.

We went from the court to a family feast at the Zoo Lake and in the evening, had a barbeque at my parents' home. I wore the same short mini and David changed into jeans for comfort. A crowd of beloved Choral Society members came. We all sat on the grass, told tall tales and sang the songs from all of our shows. Peter accompanied us on guitar. He was extravagant in his music but I pushed away my anxiety. Tonight was for us and tomorrow I would worry about Bipolar. Now under a velvet black sky with the Southern Cross keeping watch directly above, we told everyone that we were married. They cheered and raised their glasses. A couple of friends laughed, looked at each other and in stage whisper asked 'Is she pregnant?' We all had a wonderful time and we were finally pushed into our car well after midnight, sad to leave such a great party. Our night at the Braamfontein Railway Hotel was wonderfully romantic.

The following morning we returned home, packed, said goodbye to the family and headed off. As I went to the car Louisa took me aside held me at arms length 'Jill you are a married woman now. Remember all I have taught you. You must wear longer skirts you are a married woman now and keep yourself only for your husband. Go in peace and God be with you my daughter.' I wept. This longed for blessing came not from Mum but from my nanny, as usual.

We had an amazing honeymoon, traveling for three days through the semi-desert Karoo, down the beautiful Garden route and on to Cape Town in Harold. We only had one very small problem of a puncture, saved for a morning when we were within twenty metres of a petrol station where we had the tire repaired. We camped each night below a canopy of stars and as close to the beach as we could get. Cooked over open fires and befriended other travelers. The scenery was spectacular, the weather superb and our time together full of fun excitement and laughter.

After three glorious weeks, we returned to my parent's home picked up my few belongings and moved into David's tiny bedsit in Pretoria.

I started the difficult task of finding a job with an incomplete degree. I remember the exhaustion of pounding the streets for all of a week. By the end of this time, I had three possibilities but took up none because I had answered an advertisement, submitted my meager CV and applied for a town-planning job before getting married and was offered this position. I had three years of geography below my belt and could speak Afrikaans so met the minimum requirements for this administrative position. I would contribute to the management of the Pretoria's town planning code by evaluating submissions for the subdivision of residential land.

How different things were in the sixties.

Peter goes off the rails again

I sat clinging to David's hand in the darkened auditorium of the Great Hall at Wits University, my fingers digging into his palm. It was in this place that we had spent most of our time together laughing, performing and falling in love. I knew the darkness well but this time it is different.

We were here to see one of the first performances of a play called 'Die Ketter' or The Heretic written by one of my Afrikaans lecturers. An allegory set in an insane asylum. The inmates represented the white South Africans. They were sitting together in the dining hall listening to a schizophrenic talking in a maniacal, high-pitched voice about how the curtains would grow if only they believed. As I watched I was sure, the curtains grew by at least an inch.

After the performance Dave and I talked late into the night about this representation of our country and its politics as mad. About how the white population had lost all sense of reality, believing we were special and had the right to tell the rest of the world that apartheid was the only way. 'I saw the curtains grow in the performance. I am just like every other South African.'

As we spoke I became very sad my thoughts shifting to Peter and my family. The play also captured the madness that encapsulated us unequivocally. Peter's illness was an expression of the angst, mania, sorrow and utter unpredictability of my family's life. He had become the madman who orchestrated our every action. We now saw every explosion as normal despite the absolute evidence that other families lived differently.

I was utterly confused and bewilderment at Peter's illness. I loved him, felt obliged to look after his interests but I also hated his ability to control all through his illness. 'Peter is amazing. He transfixes people. They believe everything he says, however mad it is. I'm so terribly afraid of him. One day he may succeed and kill me! David I need you to understand my family and particularly Peter. Will you protect me? He is well now but I know things will change again soon.'

***

93

Peter was at university for all of a year before things spiraled out of control. This coincided with my marrying and moving away from home. Then Peter's mental health imploded because family structure changed. Family therapists eat your hearts out.

No feelings about Peter were ever simple. How could they be when his illness meant that the family and possibly others could be in danger? I always feared Peter's loss of control and wondered what new and absurd behavior would intervene.

While sad about what happened, I cannot help smiling when thinking about Peter's first vacation job. He managed ground staff at one of Johannesburg's most prestigious golf courses. In his induction, Peter was told about the difficulties keeping the grounds green. 'While you are with us, think through this problem and see if you can find a solution.'

In talking to my Dad, Peter's employer said 'We watched in awe as Peter first restructured the positions of all ground staff. His fervor was intense and his eyes shone as he went out with each worker and talked through how to improve their workflow. I became apprehensive as he thumbed feverishly though equipment manuals and placed a huge order for new equipment. When he came to me with a sketchy plan to complete redesign the golf course I decided to intervene.'

'And . . .'

'His speech was now breathless, his sentences running together. His eyes were wild and his movements jerky. My gut turned. I was dealing with a mad man. When I cautioned Peter and he rushed onto the course arms flailing and soil flying I sacked him.'

Peter, now as high and volatile as a shooting star needed hospitalization. He was admitted to Tara, a progressive open mental hospital connected to the University Medical faculty. Here he was medicated but much to the doctor's consternation and utter amazement, even huge doses did nothing to contain him and Peter's illness escalated out of control.

***

One afternoon, we visited and Peter was morose and uncommunicative. We suggested croquet as a distraction. Peter seemed to enjoy this very much. He took his time, lined up the ball and gave it a good thwack. It went through the hoop and he cheered.

As the afternoon progressed, other patients heard Peter's cheers, stopped by and two or three young men joined us on the green. Peter turned to a lanky young man of about twenty with close cropped black hair, honey colored skin and sunken dark eyes 'It's your turn Jesus.' Jesus took aim but missed. Peter took his turn and got close to but not through the hoop, sighed and handed his mallet to a stocky pugilistic teen with a matted light blond ponytail and penetrating stare. 'Your turn Jesus.'

Jesus grabbed the mallet 'I'm God's only son and I won't miss. Watch me!' He lined up the ball, crossed himself, looked towards the heavens muttered something and finally hit the ball with a solid thwack. It hit the hoop and he cursed angrily to himself. 'Better luck next time! Perhaps God is with me today. Watch and learn' said lanky Jesus 1 grabbing the mallet back.

'It's not your turn' said Jesus 2 as he turned to another inmate sitting disconsolately on the railing waiting to be included. Invited he shuffled across and waited until instructed by Peter. 'Come on Tim get going.' Tim tapped the ball and returned to his perch without looking up.

'Bless you' said Peter with a smile 'Jill it's your turn, then David.' My head spinning I took my turn.

Seeing Peter amongst these inmates, he seemed amused and utterly sane. He followed the game, chatted easily with Dave and me, kept the peace between Jesus 1 and 2 and encouraged Tim. He acted as host making sure that the game progressed easily, inclusively and without incident.

An amusing afternoon with two saviors, a shuffling downcast depressive and Peter the congenial cognoscente mad man playing against us. At the end of the game, Jesus 1 took me aside and explained that he was the messiah and Jesus 2 an imposter. 'I've been told not to mess with him because he's nuts, and anyway I didn't want to disturb the game.'

Peter smiled broadly as he waved goodbye. 'How was your holy afternoon? If you need a break I'm sure we have room for another Jesus or two.'

***

95

About a week, later Peter became depressed and stopped. The family was asked for ideas to cheer him up. I brought a couple of favorites from my parents' bookshelves trying to get Peter to read again. Sartre's 'Nausea', Camus' 'The Outsider' and Kafka's 'Metamorphosis.' When we visited the following week, his doctor took us aside and asked if we knew anything about Peter's reading choices. 'His books scare me. We'll put him on suicide watch.'

Oh what had I done? It wasn't only the books I berated myself about. He seemed so normal on our last visit. Did I trigger his behavior with the books or was it Mum and Dad? Had Mum been ranting? Was she angry? Was she worrying about politics again? Was Dad going away? My answer this time was that I was at fault. I'd moved out leaving Peter to face Mum and Dad alone. Obviously, this was too much and my fault after all.

Within two weeks of our visit, Peter was high again, hallucinating, eating anything he could get his hands on, pacing the ward and grounds, pushing people aside, talking loudly and fighting anyone who attempted to medicate him. He ran away to a supermarket where he ate food off the shelves and became angry when challenged by the owner. The police were called and Peter was placed in a locked ward. Here he finally collapsed into a depression so deep he became catatonic. The doctors could describe Peter's symptoms but offered no diagnosis. They had no clue about treatment. Mum was devastated.

Taking a break from flat-hunting and my new job in Pretoria, I visited and Peter's whole body was as stiff as a board. I tried to move his outstretched hand but couldn't bend it. He was rigid. He stared straight ahead and said nothing.

'Peter please say something, anything. Come on we've come a long way to spend time with you. Please! . . Peter where are you?'

When his medication did nothing to bring Peter out of his depression, the doctors added a full course of ECT and when even shock treatment failed, they persuaded my parents to consent to trialing a new treatment still in an experimental phase. Psychiatric medicine had nothing else to offer. They would now use Insulin Shock Therapy (IST) to reset Peter's brain.

For eight weeks, Peter was injected with large doses of insulin to produce daily comas six days a week. The doctors hoped this would jolt him out catatonia and speed up remission. No further explanation was offered.

We visited week after week to see the shell of Peter propped up in bed, jaw hanging loose, vacant stare and saying nothing. The light had gone out. Any sign of Peter lost.

I was terrified. My brother Peter was gone. After each visit, I left speechless, tears welling as David reached for my hand when his words went unanswered. I'd avoid Mum and Dad go strait back to Pretoria, climb into a hot bath and stair at the ceiling before crawling into bed where I'd cry myself to sleep.

***

My feelings about Peter had always been ambivalent. I felt warm and close to him as a small child but jealous because he was super intelligent and I felt dumb. I was always immensely moved by Peter's music but scared because he tried to kill me. Who was Peter and what was his illness? A persona in its own right? He'd always been larger than life and now he did nothing. Didn't move, blank stare, no response at all, he wasn't there and I was without hope.

I wish I could have captured and held for a moment the part of Peter who was before IST. After, my beautiful sensitive brother with his extravagant range of emotions was gone leaving only the husk or shell. Vanished and without his responding I couldn't connect. Peter had become a great big lumbering wreck who could not laugh, cry or relate; as if he lived behind a glass wall and only Mum's devastating rage could shatter this screen. Now a clatter and banging of Peter's discordant mutterings were his only response; any residual light was hidden behind a straightjacket of pills.

Mum, Dad, Dave and I all challenged the doctors. Dad made appointment after appointment with Peter's psychiatrist who would simply throw his hands in the air and say it takes time and in some cases, nothing changes. When Mum screamed and demanded more, the doctor turned to her and said 'We are doing what we can, if you have anything to add go ahead. We have exhausted all our options.'

Dad took over and asked if there were other hospital that could do better. 'If it needs money I'll find it. Please where can we take him?'

'We are a research hospital and up with the rest of the world. Sometimes there are no answers. Not everything can be fixed by throwing money at it.'

When we visited, Peter did not acknowledge us. Each conversation was stillborn.

'Hi Peter. How are you?'

Peter stared straight past us. I tried again 'I've had a busy week. We've found a flat. Perhaps you can come over some time.'

Peter didn't move as he mumbled 'flat.'

Dave tried 'Have you played any chess this week Peter?'

Peter echoed 'chess.'

'Yup learned any new moves?' Nothing.

'Would you like to go for a walk?' Nothing.

'Come on Pete, the nurse said it'd be good to walk a bit.' Dave reached for Peter and pulled gently until he was upright 'A few steps. Outside perhaps.' Peter's socked feet dragged along the floor and then he slowly shuffled into motion hovered and stopped as he collided with a chair turned ninety degrees and shuffled forward again an automaton whose circuitry was burned out. He was now not that different from my robot vacuum cleaner that moves towards an object until it bumps and then turns and moves off in another direction.

Accept it - Peter is disabled

After another couple of months, Peter went home. I visited and as I came down the path to the front door, I heard the strangled yowl of a cat. I rushed inside to find Peter pulling hard at the cat's head. I grabbed at his arm. He let the cat go and grabbed my hair. I was drawn close and screamed into his face hovering expressionless in front of me. Pulled away leaving a handful of hair in Peter's clenched fist and ran to the kitchen looking for Louisa's help. He slowly got to his feet and lumbered after me. I ran out of the back door. He stopped on the top step. I cried out but no one answered so I ran for the car where I shivered, then slowly calmed myself and drove off. The fear was back and the constant nagging feeling that if only I had been able to reach out and touch him before his ICT it would not have been necessary to kill his spirit. How I missed you Peter. If only I'd known the secret to hold your soul.

Mum begged me to come again the following weekend. 'Will you be home, because I'm scared of Peter?'

When I arrived, Mum and Dad were in the lounge sitting side by side and Peter was nowhere to be seen. As Dave and I entered, they looked up but didn't say anything.

'Hi! Where's Peter?'

'He's back in hospital. We couldn't cope.'

Mum rubbed her hands together as if she were washing them. She was crying silently and I was petrified. I was used to anger and noise but not this hopeless whimper.   I turned my gaze on Dad. 'What did we do wrong Jill? What happened?'

I sat, chest pounding and breathing heavily. My mind was full of uncontrolled thoughts 'Shit, this is my fault, I shouldn't have left. Peter was OK until I got married.'

Dave intervened. 'Have the doctors said anything?'

Dad shook his head 'They've tried everything.'

We sat in silence for a long time and then Dad suggested. 'Dave perhaps you can come with me to the hospital.'

They left and Mum and I wept together. Mum moaning over and over again 'This can't be happening, my beautiful boy. This can't be happening.'

I was silent.

***

When Peter came home, again he was zombie-like and compliant. I let go of hope and thought about my responsibility for helping Mum and Dad manage the behaviour of this burned-out wreck, my brother.

Now the family had to acknowledge that a disabled Peter needed to accept his condition and find a way to live in the world. Dad went to work planning for Peter's future and what follows is David's recollection of a meeting he had with Dad and Dr. Hart, Peter's psychiatrist.

First steps through the looking glass world

Not long after Jill's family had accepted me, her father, Hans, asked me if I could meet with him and Doctor Hart, Peter's psychiatrist. I always found Hans hard to read, but he was unusually serious, and exuded a hint of excitement. I agreed to come.

Doctor Hart and Hans were already talking when I arrived that afternoon, but only in general terms about politics and the state of Peter's health. Peter was at Tara, an open psychiatric hospital, receiving treatment at the time, so was not home. Oddly, we met in Hans' bedroom, rather than the living room, but it was a comfortable space.

Hans kicked off the meeting by saying how concerned he was about Peter's future now that it did not look as if he would ever complete his education or be able to hold down a reasonably paid job. Further, he would not always be around to rescue Peter. To address this he had set up a trust that would guarantee Peter a reasonable income for the rest of his life. Any residue at Peter's death would pass to Jill, or to her children if there were any at that time. The initial trustees would be himself, Doctor Hart, Mr. C who was an accountant and financial advisor, and he hoped that I would be willing to be a trustee as well.

100

Doctor Hart was taken aback by this proposal, as it had not been discussed with him at all before it was set up. He immediately expressed his concern that this arrangement would work against Peter's interests, as Peter's main task over the next few years was to learn to be self-sufficient because the chance of a cure or extended remission was unlikely. Knowing that he was cared for would undermine his incentive to work at this.

He did not use these words, but Doctor Hart appeared to be saying that it was like giving an alcoholic a live-in carer to make sure he would never need to take the consequences for his drinking. I did not have the knowledge or experience of Doctor Hart, but there was a churning feeling deep in my gut that he was right and what Hans was doing was wrong in some way.

Hans' response to our reluctance was to put on his best sales manner and try to sell all of the benefits to us, but we were adamant. Doctor Hart because he felt it undermined Peter, and I because I trusted Doctor Hart's judgment. The meeting ended with Hans reluctantly agreeing to a compromise, where the Trust would remain in place, but Peter was never to be told of its existence. Hart left, and I stayed back as I had been invited to dinner.

Over dinner Hans recounted his decision to set up the Trust, and our meeting with Doctor Hart, to Else and Jill. He was particularly pleased that Doctor Hart supported the Trust and felt it would benefit Peter by taking a load off his mind. Hans could not wait to tell Peter about it.

Dad set up a trust that would care for Peter financially for the rest of his life. He chose an executor to watch over the trust and appointed Dr. Hart as a trustee.

LEAVING HOME

In leaving my parent's home, I believe I am formally taking responsibility for my own life. Now I can decide how to move forward, find agency, be my own woman. The irony is that despite thinking this, I am happy and confident that David is now my legal protector.

***

South Africa in 1970 is well set up to support any new wife willing to lean on her man. I move from my father's house to be with my husband. I need his permission to have a bank account but am free to work with his blessing for a woman's wage, which was about 15% below a man's, until I have children. Then I am expected to stay home and care for my family.

There is no safety net for women in South Africa. Once they marry and move from their father's house, they become the husband's responsibility. All her possessions become his and if the relationship breaks down or the husband becomes bankrupt, these assets are seen as the husband's. Women are very vulnerable in such situations. My father worries about my financial position under South African law so gives us a pre-nuptial contract as a wedding gift. This protects me from possible destitution if David leaves me. I don't think much about what Dad is doing because I am confident in my relationship and don't think beyond the present, but I like the promise of a home and a Scottish terrier, my favorite of all dogs, if David either goes bankrupt or leaves me.

David gladly takes on the role of defender and is solicitous when I seek his succor. He cannot however save me from myself and, while I forgot my fears in the close-knit University community, a new life in conservative Pretoria is challenging. Throughout our courtship, there was no situation where I had to approach people or build relationships on my own so we were both shocked by my phobia. What am I so scared of?

I stumble and stutter as I search for something to say. People will see me hide behind a blank, silent mask. They will find nothing to connect with and walk away.

When David begins introducing me to work colleagues I am overwhelmed by their geekish intelligence and literally hide behind him when expected to mix. He hasn't seen this behavior before and is initially gentle and solicitous. He asks what's going on, assures me that people want to meet me, asks how he can help and allows me time to adjust. After several months, he begins to push for an occasional out. He wants more freedom to relax and indulge his extrovert self free of my clinging.

He obviously finds me exhausting as transfixed by fear I stand on the edge of any gathering and wait for a reasonable time to drag David away. This in turn builds my anxiety. I am impossible and perhaps he will leave.

***

Soon after moving to Pretoria, we decide that David's bed-sit is too small and find a larger flat. I remember so well this cozy new home, which becomes our haven. We furnish it with great care. I consider each item and its place and slowly produce a picture perfect whole.

Each time I enter, I stop on the doorstep, allow my eyes to readjust to the brightness of our lovely living room. I breathe in the aroma of perfumed flowers in a vase atop my tallboy, which stands in pride of place against the stark white wall. The flowers reflect back from the depth of the polished surface of the drawers. My eyes move first to the sleek modern dining table and chairs and then down to a lovely woven rug in muted mustard, vermilion and purple. My gaze then moves beyond to the snug sitting space, out through full-length windows framed by curtains the color of burnt toffee and across the valley to the Union buildings, The white walls show our two Katz paintings and a number of prints off to perfection. I am so proud of what we've created.

A new life begins, but my issues with Peter, my self-doubt and my fear still persists.

Will Peter ever let me be

Munitoria, my first workplace, a seven-storied labyrinth of identical corridors covering a full city block is the fulfillment of Kafka's *Castle*; the work carried out within its walls a manifestation of this mammoth maze. Here rules and policies for the administration of the city of Pretoria are conceived, overseen and micro-managed.

I am comfortable at work because, for the first time I can remember, everything is contained, ordered and manageable. Wonderful in light of Peter's returning illness and my wish to establish a new private life in Pretoria. There are ten people in my section, and I am only expected to mix with the two other girls doing comparable work. My boss understands that I want to finish my degree and there is free time for study.

My job entails seeing whether planned subdivisions of land comply with the Land Act's zoning, use, size and the provision of services such as water, electricity and rates. My role is circumscribed, but service users well schooled in the art of 'getting things through council' openly suggest incentives. Interestingly, they don't appeal to my material interests, but David's. 'Does your husband like whisky? I bought you this special blend. It is just a little thank you for your help.'

'But sir I'm well paid.'

'Ah yes but this might just help you to get my application through smoothly.'

'Sir if your surveyor has carried out his work correctly there'll be no problem.'

'Well it's a good whisky. Your husband does enjoy a drink doesn't he?'

When I speak about it at home, Dave laughs 'You know I love a good tipple but I'm pleased you stand up to them.'

'Ah well this way I'll be able to the hold the high moral ground and Kingsmead won't have gone completely to waste.

Dave chuckles.

Later I am given a greater diversity of work related to the planning of new suburbs. As my immediate boss, a twenty-year veteran, grows to trust me, he spends less time at work. I'm happy with the increased authority. During lunch break, I play poker with the land development guys and take David who works half an hour away in Silverton to the movies each week on 'my losses.' I have learned when playing poker in Choral Society not to show my winnings and with nothing on the table, I fool the very macho crew 'Can you afford to play?' Strange, don't they know how much money they lose?

***

I have been in my job eight months when Peter arrives at work unannounced having taken a day pass from hospital. To my surprise, he has remembered where I work. He waves extravagantly, strides down the corridor, fly open and hair sticking out in all directions, twirling a two liter coke bottle.

'Oh shit!'

'Hi Jill, like where you work.' He turns to open a door. I grab his arm and steer him toward my office.

'I'm starving. Got anything for me to eat? Where's your boss? I'm here to check up on you.'

'In here.' I rush him into my office and close the door.

'Sit and do up your fly . . . um . . . I'll phone Dave.' I turn to the phone and dial. 'Hi Dave, Peter is here can you come' and then I whisper 'Quickly please!'

'OK! I'll need to let people know, and my experiment . . . I'll find someone to watch it and be there as soon as I can.'

'Thanks.'

I hang up and turn to Peter who is pacing up and down the office. 'I was thirsty 'cause I hitched a ride on the back of a pickup. It took an hour . . . Hot with the wind in my face so I took a Coke off the back of a delivery truck. The driver saw and gave chase. Lucky we were close to Munitoria so I dashed in before he could catch me, ran up the stairs and escaped. Any ice?'

'Hope no one saw you. If the police are after you I won't be able to hide you from my bosses.'

'Why'd you want to do that?'

'This is my work place Peter.'

Dave comes more quickly than I think possible, knocks, comes in and closes the door behind him.

'Hi' he comes behind my desk and kisses me.

'Hi. Sorry I need the loo. I'll be back in a second.' Thank God Dave is here to watch Peter.

Dave turns to Peter 'What're you doing here?'

'Came to see how Jill's going at work. Thought I might chat with her boss. See how she's doing.'

'Right.' Dave sits and persuades Peter to do the same. 'Jill's not supposed to have visitors at work and I'm not sure her boss would speak to you.'

'But . . .' Peter gets agitated.

'Come on Pete let's head home. You haven't seen where we live. Have you? Just hang on a sec and I'll be back.' Dave pops out into the passage, peaks both ways comes back and says 'See you at home if you can get away Jill', steers Peter out of the room, down to the lifts and out. As they disappear a customer comes to the counter, clearly he saw Peter and Dave at the lift as he looks back over his shoulder and shakes his head before ringing for service.

I dash back into my corridor, breathe, walk across the passage and knock at my boss's door. He looks up 'Have you finished already?'

'Um . . . no. It's . . . I'm really nauseous and I've got a headache. Is it OK to go home? I'll catch up tomorrow.'

'You were fine half an hour ago and we've got that meeting'

'Please?'

'Well if you must. Let me know if you're still sick in the morning and remember to fill in a sick day.'

'Thanks.'

I walk slowly back to the office, close the door, rush to my desk, grab my bag and leave. When I'm out of the building, I sigh 'Thank God!'

When I get home, Peter is throwing the cat at the ceiling. 'Landed on your feet that time Alexis.' Dave steps forward and puts his hand on Peter's shoulder. Peter pushes back his face now a nose away from Dave's and raises his voice 'But Dave I'm just trying to work out how many centimetres a cat needs to right himself and fall on his feet.'

'Peter stop now!'

Peter doesn't listen, gets out of Dave's grip, grabs Alexis and hurls him at the ceiling again. Alexis yowls, Peter cackles and David steps forward, but even with Dave holding him Peter turns, grabs the escaping Alexis and hurls him at the floor. I grab Alexis and run crying into the bedroom terrified for my beautiful kitten. He looks up at me and purrs. Just as I go to close the door Peter is there. Alexis sees him, wriggles out of my arms, hisses, runs for the kitchen, and escapes through the milk hatch. Peter with arms hanging limp from his shoulders, turns, goes into the lounge and sits.

We follow and Dave says to Peter 'We really care about you Pete but you can't just drop in on Jill at work. Next time you want to come over, give us a call and we'll come and fetch you. If we know you're coming we can prepare, maybe make a meal or take you out.' I sit silent knowing that Dave is wasting his breath. Peter won't listen. He can't. The circuitry is bust. He'll just keep doing what he wants to do.

We drive Peter back to Tara, Peter's new home from home. As we leave, Peter is still hanging out of his window, 'Bye Dave. Bye Jill. I'll visit again soon.'

'Oh please God no. I don't want him to ruin the new life. Please!'

Alexis only reappears when we come home from work the following evening. He hides every time Peter visits. There are many more visits but few as difficult. Thank heavens.

***

This night-horror is as clear, stark, and frightening as when it happened after Peter's visit. I get up half asleep and head for the toilet. As I leave our bedroom a shadowy creature crouches against the wall ready to pounce and I scream. David jumps up and is immediately at my side. Alexis also as I shake, heart pounding and lungs completely starved of air. David puts his

107

arms around me, turns the light on and I see that the apparition is nothing more than a lovely vase of flowers arranged on my special tallboy.

Slowly the pounding recedes and after a warm cocoa I return to bed and cuddle close to David. I don't sleep for a long while, as I remember the resonating horrors from my childhood. Now, I can only remember the terror followed by the watching.

I had so hoped that my nightmares would stop when I left my parents' home but here they are full-blown and horrifying. If only . . . Well they're not leaving so grit your teeth and get on with it girl. At least you have a life.

Cancer

My connection with Mum grows as we share our sadness. We phone regularly and talk about day-to-day trivialities. 'The roses are beautiful. Tom got the pruning just right this year.'

'I miss having a garden.'

'Well come on Saturday and have dinner; we can eat alfresco'

'Sounds great, how's work? Sell anything lately?'

'A beautiful tourmaline pendant to a crinkly old fart.' We avoid talking about Peter because nothing has changed and that's hard to face. How can we come to terms with having no hope for Peter? Our grief draws us closer as Mum talks about her pain and depression. 'I can't get to sleep at night, have continual indigestion and Gin has lost its potency.'

When we camp together in the mountains, it's different. Mum drinks less; we talk about her past and my future, about Fascism, freedom and new frontiers and sing together. As we sit by a mountain stream, I take Mum's hand and thank her for my schooling and the wonderful trip to Europe. She looks at her feet and says sorry for the times she forgot or hurt me as she fought her pain and trauma. And then before I know it the moment is gone, Mum has stripped to her skin, and her sleek body shimmers as she dives into a crystal clear pool just a metre away. She is as always a sight to be seen.

Louisa notices a difference our relationship and draws me aside on one visit. 'It is good that you and your mother speak. I worry about her. She is much quieter. Her life is running away and she's sad. It's good that you are kind to her.' I smile encouraged by her constant vigilance.

'And Peter, Louisa, how do you find him?'

'He is not with us Miss Jill. He's run away. Only his body is here and we are all sad for him.'

'Yes Louisa we are.' I hug her. She voices her sadness so easily. If only we were like her, always wise and down to earth. 'Thanks Louisa' I smile and decide to visit Johannesburg more often. It is good to home.

Not long after my chat with Louisa, I get a call from Dad. 'Else is in hospital and asking to see you.' When I get there, I'm told 'She's had a partial mastectomy, has cancer and they didn't get it all.'

'But you don't just get cancer. What happened Mum?'

'I found a lump a year ago but with Peter I just couldn't face any more so ignored it. By the time I got to the doctor I needed breast surgery.'

Mum always proud of her lithe athletic body, didn't want her breast removed so they cut a great hunk away leaving a grotesque contorted nipple. A badly burned relic of what was once a beautiful curve. When the bandages come off Mum asks me to look. She lifts her blouse and I see scorched flesh and seared skin pulled tight into a scarred distorted teat. 'I didn't want to loose my nipple but it's not the same. It's hideous isn't it.' Mum turns her sunken pale face towards me and I know from the look in her piercing blue eyes that she has caught me before I could guard what I felt. I am devastated by what I see. Somehow, this hideous scar brings the word cancer to life. Mum was so ill that the only way to hang on was to hack away at her handsome body, one of the few things she treasured. 'You hate it don't you? ...' She sniffs away the tears 'I'm losing everything I care about. Do you think they can fix it with an implant.'

What can I say? I'm scared for her life and she's worried about the way she looks. I excuse myself and rush to the loo. I need time to get myself together to be there for her. The sight of breast has sickened me. It is ugly, no grotesque, burned, and misshaped. Nothing will fix it. How do I hide my feelings? Having found a gentler relationship with Mum for the first time, I begin to think about her dying.

Slowly Mum begins to smile again. 'Margo says I have to take it easy so I'm spending less time at work and she's offered to take me to chemo. This regime is grueling and within weeks, Mum has lost all her hair. Margo buys her a wig but it looks ridiculous after Mum's crop of unruly hair so she does without. Her shining pate suits her and gradually a downy soft grey fluff starts to cover her head and Mum looks lovely. Her face is much gentler without the wiry mop. Each week she gets stronger. For a while, Dad is solicitous and Peter is kept at a distance. I come over often and finally Mum begins camping again. Now used to the scar she decides against the implant.

Dad is back at camp preparing the evening meal, we sit by a stream in the warm sum of a late afternoon, and Mum turns to me and asks. 'Do you mind? I want to swim, can you bear to look?'

I rise and strip. 'Sure.'

What a change. Before she flaunted herself, now she is asking timidly for my approval. How life's changed.

This is one of the very few times we spend together without Peter and it's so peaceful. We're almost a normal loving family facing a difficult illness together. But of course, this is foolishness, merely a reprieve. Tomorrow I'll go back to Pretoria, and Mum and Dad will go home to the tension of Peter's illness. He's at Tara again, his behavior florid. Mum being ill has set him off again and Dr Hart has agreed that she needs a break. With Peter in hospital for a couple of weeks, it is quieter at home but of course out of sight does not mean out of mind where Peter is concerned.

***

David speaks to me about Mum's illness. 'Having a grandchild while she is well enough to enjoy the experience is something you can give your mum. It might keep her going a little longer.' I am terrified about having a schizophrenic child and afraid that I don't have what it takes to be a mother.

'I'm scared. I'm not sure I want children at all. What if they're mad like Peter?'

'Shall we chat with the doctor. I'm pretty sure Schizophrenia isn't genetic. I've done lots of reading and . . . '

'Going to the doctor won't help and I don't like kids anyway. I told you that before we married. I'll be the one at home not you and I don't think I've got it in me. I don't want any kid to feel the way I did growing up.'

Dave lets the discussion drop but revisits it the following evening.

'I've done some more reading and there is some association of mental illness in families but no genetic proof.'

'I'm scared of kids and have no mothering instincts what so ever.'

'That'll come when the baby's your own.'

'Mum's not so keen on kids either. I think this is a bad idea.'

'Jill I want kids so what about my feelings. I'll help. It'll be OK.'

I hear David's plea so finally swallow both concerns and try to fall pregnant. Within a month, I've conceived.

Not one to follow convention I don't leave work until the day before I give birth. My larger responsibilities at work include on site visits so I heave my huge tummy through fences as I carry on without concessions to my condition. Contractions begin in bed the night after I leave and in the bank queue the following morning, my waters break. Dave drives me to hospital and within an hour, I'm in labor. A battered and bruised Richard is forced into the world between forceps a good twenty-four hours later and I'm exhausted. Richard's huge nose dominates his face and he looks pretty much like Harold our VW; but despite his looks, I'm overwhelmed with love for this ugly little monster. When he's placed in my arms I cry and say 'did I do this' and an overjoyed Dave holds my hand and tells me I'm wonderful. He's thrilled that we have produced the first son who will carry the family name Richard, which is passed on from generation to generation.

I am panic-stricken when the nurses take Richard and put him in a humidicrib because he had trouble taking his first breath. For two days, I spend most of my waking hours creeping painfully up and down the corridor to peak at him. Mum comes to visit on day three and all I remember is her hurtful if genuine words.

'My God he's ugly.'

Having Richard is wonderful and I love him, but feel like an unfit mother. He is born placenta praevia and I don't produce milk so am immediately confronted with my inadequacies. I hate being stuck at home and don't know what to do with Richard or myself. On formula, he guzzles down his bottle, then writhes, and screams as his stomach churns. When nothing changes by the third month, I take him to the doctor who says I am a new mother and just need to relax. I am mortified.

I come home with Richard crying in the back of the car, take him inside and try to pacify him. He won't calm so I change his nappy. It's another runny, pooey mess and his nappy will come out of the wash a poo yellow color because I can't even get washing right. I try singing to him, he is quiet for a moment, then writhes and cries again. I can hear the bubbles in his gut but I don't know what to do. I put him down and walk out. He keeps on crying and I can't bear it so I go back into his room, pick him up and yell 'stop.' Betsy the next-door neighbor, who is a social worker hears me through our open back door and her open window and rushes in, obviously concerned that I'm about to throw him at the wall. She takes him and tells me to go and rest. I am so grateful.

For three whole months, Richard does not sleep through the night and cries incessantly through the day. Every time he cries I feel my brain sizzle as I struggle not to hurt my child. Each time Dave arrives home, I shove Richard into his arms and run for the safety of the street and walk until my head stops jangling.

David talks to other fathers at work and also searches through articles on colic. I ask everyone I meet and finally the answer comes from a colleague of Dave's. Richard is lactose intolerant in a country where such conditions are rare. We try soymilk and finally the bubbles slow down and Richard begins to smile.

I enjoy Richard's relief for a little while and then another problem raises its ugly head. I am shy and since my encounter with the dentist in the psych hospital at twelve, I have always found closeness difficult. Sex is one thing but to cuddle and kiss or merely to let another stretch out and touch me brings a stiffness to my spine. I freeze, watch and wait. I wait for the bile to rise up the back of my throat, for the insistent threat of nausea, for the fear of being overcome. This struggle won't leave me. Where others greet with an embrace I cannot. Where another may take someone's arm, I stand solid and rooted to the ground as my eyes plead please don't touch.

Now that Richard is not wracked with pain, he wants to cuddle and reaches out in love so I swallow back on that bile and fight to learn closeness. This doesn't come, even as others say 'It will! Mothering is natural just take your time'. So I wait as my Richard tries to draw me close. He gurgles and stretches his little arms towards me but I find it almost impossible. I cannot be so close. Not even with him. One of my fears is well and truly realized as I struggle to mother.

I push a pram disconsolately around the suburb, wondering what the hell I'm doing and how I'd got myself into this serfdom, when I'm greeted on our closest corner by a lady whose husband digs in the garden behind her. She rushes out of her property and pokes her head into the pram. 'What a beautiful baby! Can I have a cuddle?' scoops Richard into her arms and extends a hand. 'Hi I'm Des and we just moved here from Grahamstown.' Thus begins a wonderful friendship. Without this lady, I would have lost the plot.

With Des, I learn a new and different way of being. She is totally without self-absorption, full of curiosity and candor and everyone loves her. She does not judge herself or others. This she leaves to God. She simply smiles and offers whoever comes another cup of tea. She has been a Christian all her life and is curious about my Jewish background. 'How can you be a Jew who doesn't believe?' I spend many hours with Des, drinking tea, chatting, watching over Richard and her three older children and learning how to be a mother. She tells me she struggled with her first for a while she before she learned to love him. I feel understood, we become close buddies and begin to spend some part of most days together. We chat, walk, cook and shop but most important we often laugh together. It's through her and her church that I make many friends.

I learn with encouragement from Dave and with Des' gentle instruction how to love my baby. I see Des cuddle Richard along her arm or sometimes she plays with him on a blanket on the floor. This way he is not so close. Dave begins to handle him more robustly, lifting Richard above his head or sitting opposite so that there is a space between them and they can enjoy passing things to each other. Richard grabs something and shoves it in his mouth for a good chew but then takes it out and moves it from hand to hand and Dave says 'good boy.' I try these simple activities and forget myself as I learn to enjoy Richard's constant babbling, enthusiasm for language, the world and all that is in it. I begin to take pride in my son. Because he spends so much time with Des's crew, he mimics them and this accelerates his learning. I'm such a proud mum and I so want to do it well.

Dave and I decide we want another child as close to Richard in age as possible. This way we can get over the work of babies as quickly as possible. I become pregnant immediately.

At eight months, Richard stands on my knees, looks me directly in the eye and stretches out his little hands to touch my nose. I gag and turn my face to the side. He leans in towards my cheek and strokes his face against mine. I fight nausea, put him down and dash for the loo. At first I think I'm ill because of being pregnant, or perhaps it's a reaction to my hormones being all over the place; but when it happens again and again, and only when Richard leans in close, I know that I cannot handle the intimacy my little one longs for. I can't talk to anyone about what's happening. I'm back in the abyss with the Boogieman, unreachable and out of control. My worst fears realized; I cannot mother and I'm pregnant again.

Dave notices my agitation and says 'You're pregnant again too soon. What can I do to help?'

'Nothing!' He is sympathetic. He knows how hard it has always been for me to cuddle and kiss him but when I try to talk this through, I become overwhelmed. 'I don't want to understand. I just want to be a normal mum.'

My fight to conquer the unwelcome phantoms from my past becomes all-consuming. I manage to stay with Richard through the day but thrust him into David's arms as he walks through the door at night, and run for my sanity into the street and away from the suffocating well of overwhelming feelings. How can I possibly manage another child?

***

Mum adores Richard and spends as much time as she can with him. Chemotherapy has halted the cancer for a while and she spends every spare moment with her grandson. They laugh and babble together, with Mum often leaning towards Richard and sharing with him secrets only known to grannies and their curly-haired grandchildren.

Mum buys Richard a magnificent wooden rocking horse and Richard sees it before his grandfather can bring it inside. He toddles out through the sliding door and, as Hans bends to say hello, grabs at the wrapping. 'What dat?'

Mum bends down and whispers in Richards ear. 'It's a wooden horse just for you.' His big brown eyes shin with excitement, he helps his grandmother strip away the paper wrapping and within seconds, he is on his horse and rocking for all he's worth. Mum is hardly in the door but she drops to the floor and sits facing Richard who chortles at his granny. Locked in a world of their own, the two of them laugh and rock and then Mum begins to sing. Richard stands astride his magnificent steed and tries to sing along. The rhythm is robust; they are totally connected and oblivious to anyone else. I am overjoyed that I took the grave risk of having a child. He is like Peter in that he is as bright as a button but he doesn't have any of the quirkiness I remember. Thank God.

I tell Mum that I am pregnant again and she is excited, but by the time Lisa is born, the chemo has failed and she is too ill to enjoy my new gift. Each time she reaches out for her new granddaughter I see fear in her eyes, 'What if I drop her? I am so tired. She is very beautiful but I'm beyond loving. I'm too sore and scared.'

Peter does not register my pregnancy as he is ill, and in hospital for the first few months of Richard's life, so Dave and I decide he should not meet his nephew.

When David does bring Peter to visit Richard in Pretoria at about ten months he is interested but a little distant. He makes no attempt to approach or speak to his new nephew and I'm apprehensive and quickly find an excuse to put Richard down to rest.

I'm relieved when David takes Peter back to Tara.

The next time he sees Richard, Peter is more settled in himself and Richard is more fun. He's a toddler and quite talkative and Peter is fascinated.

Again, I'm vigilant but as Richard enjoys his uncle, I don't whisk him away. Peter notices that we won't leave him alone with

Richard and comments 'You won't leave us alone, well fair enough I guess I can't be trusted.'

***

Lisa is born just fifteen months after Richard and my body and mind aren't ready for this beautiful new addition to the family.

At birth, Richard had been misshapen but Lisa born after only six hours has the tiniest pixy face, a slim little body and beautiful long fingers and toes. I see and recognized Dave in her long limbs but the bullet round head and cherub face with big eyes are mine. I'm so proud and determined I'll feed this mite myself and not give up as I did with Richard. Her smile comes soon, her temperament is gentle and accommodating, and yet within a few days of her birth I'm weeping uncontrollably.

David tries to comfort me, thanking me for our beautiful children and reminding me how much my now very ill mother adores these little people, but nothing will stop my crying. I don't feel sad but my continual weeping belies this. I go to the doctor whose only advice is that it will pass. David invites the minister to visit and he prays for my soul but still I cry. Postnatal depression has no name in 1975 so I cry and cry. Lisa, oblivious to the distress others feel keeps nuzzling into my breast and drinking well until suddenly one day my crying stops and life continues.

Church, Community and Politics

Des and Mike become close friends and I keep pushing Mike on how he, a geologist or any other right-minded person of our generation, can believe in creationism and the possibility of a present and involved God. 'You believe that the world was created in seven days?'

'I don't.'

Mike is as monosyllabic as Des is chatty. He believes not only in God but also that his 'Yes should be yes and no, no!' so any conversation is deliberate and circumscribed. After months of my confronting Mike and him giving short precise answers, I accept that I can believe in both God and evolution and go with them to church. His comment 'We all have faith, mine is in God and yours is perhaps in your intellect but each of us believes' resonates.

My rebirth as a Christian is wonderful and inevitable. I find the sermons continually challenge me to accept my past, forgive those who have hurt me, seek forgiveness myself where I have hurt others and use my experiences to seek justice and help others. I begin to feel I am part of an involved plan leading towards an inevitable victory through Christ who takes my burdens upon Himself.

I become deeply involved with the church community. Five church families live within a city block and we spend much time together, share childrearing, communion in the form of many meals together and supporting each other in daily living. Wonderful as this is, being a homemaker with no involvement in the real world excruciating. I feel disconnected and because very few white mothers work until their children are at school I begin looking for something worthwhile to do. Politics can be done alongside child rearing.

My church mates and particularly Des are happy to help with the kids, so I volunteer with the Progressive Federal Party (PFP).

The FFP believes in broadening the franchise to include other races. Julie who registers me as a member immediately invites me into the office in the back room of a small house owned by a couple of Jewish lefties. Francis and her basset hound greet us at the door. We soon became good friends and I learn that she has no desire to have children but chose to work from home. She is a freelance journalist. The office is neat and accessible but small.

Over the next year and a half, Julie, tall, generous, determined, cynical and full of laughter and I work hard to drum up business. By the end of this time, we have a well functioning outfit that has outgrown the small office. We move the budding administrative center into Mary's garage. She is an organizational powerhouse and loves detecting so takes charge of the cards and the voter roll and begins searching out voter's affiliations. Mary is a superb sleuth and uses previous connections to find out about and classify voters. Julie and I handle logistics.

We lived in the nation's capital and the PFP wanted to put up a candidate in the next election despite knowing that actually winning a seat was only the faintest of possibilities. When a by-election is held in the seat of Waterkloof, we put up a candidate.

We begin campaigning with a small group of volunteers who are willing to canvas door to door; to spend at least one afternoon or evening a week visiting voters we have tagged as open and talk with them about voting for the PFP. If there is no hope, we move on quickly and change their card to 'against'. If they need more persuading, we add them to the list of those to be visited again. Our number of volunteers increases as others see our enthusiasm. When the election takes place we double our vote. We are delighted and when the government sees the swing, they redraw the boundaries of our electorate. For the first time our presence had been registered.

Peter's visits are still scary

Peter's first introductions to Richard went OK but I never take anything with him for granted. He had attacked me and now I am concerned that he might harm my children. However, Peter is my flesh and blood and has little to celebrate in his own life so who am I to deny him the happiness of getting to know the garrulous, inquisitive Richard and his gentle but already determined baby sister Lisa.

***

Peter is larger than life. He loves his nephew and his tiny niece, so visits often. When he first meets Richard, he actually acknowledges my concern and says he understands my anxiety and I try not to be too obviously paranoid. Protecting myself is one thing, but looking after my little ones when he is around is another. While I have wondered what I might have done to trigger Peter, I am clear that Richard is blameless, innocent and vulnerable.

When Peter comes with Mum and Dad to meet Lisa for the first time he is again full of trepidation. He smiles at Richard 'Hi Rich what have you got. A little sister?'

Richard immediately takes Peter to another part of the room to look at a trolley he loves and Peter spends the rest of the visit playing on the floor with the trolley, Richard and the cat. Hidey swishes her tail, which Richard grabs and Peter laughs and watches.

When Dad says they need to go about an hour later Peter said 'Bye' to Richard, ignores me and Lisa, who is feeding, and wanders off to the car with Dave and my parents. From that time on Peter visits with my parents occasionally. Neither Richard nor Lisa are concerned by him. Instead, they seem captivated.

Despite this easy relationship I never invite Peter when I am alone with the children because I still do not trust either him or myself without the support of the family.

***

Richard is fascinated as Peter arrives very high one afternoon and demands to be fed. David digs out some mince and begins to make a bolognaise sauce but Peter cannot wait. He wolfs down slice after slice of a loaf of bread. Richard watches his hand traveling towards and away from his mouth, mimicking Peter as he clearly tries to comprehend what he's doing. Then Peter grabs a spoon and starts shoveling raw mince from the pan as it defrosts and Richard's Jaw drops. 'Daddy, Uncle Peter's naughty! He's eating raw meat!'

'I'm hungry.'

Richard steps between Peter and the pan. 'We don't eat raw meat?'

'Well I do.'

'Daddy. Peter's got bad manners.'

'It's OK Rich! How's your Lego house?'

'You're funny Peter. Do you want to see my house?'

'When I've eaten!'

Richard goes off to play, still mimicking Peter. David chuckles and cooks and I watch gob smacked as Peter continues to stuff his face. Luckily, it's Saturday and David is here. He takes Peter in his stride. 'Peter, Jill and I are taking the kids out. We are bathing them and then we'll be off.'

'It's OK, I'll come with you.'

'It's a kid's party Peter. I'll take you back and join Jill later.' David turns to me. 'You go ahead.'

I sigh. Thank God for Dave; without him I wouldn't cope with Peter. 'Thanks I'll take them now and you can join us later.'

The Black Sash

In the PFP I meet an old mate, May, vibrant, passionate and gentle who invites me to a meeting of the Black Sash and I'm reminded that it's not only a protest movement. Many Black Sashers volunteer in a national network of advice offices, a visible proof of white resistance towards the apartheid system. At the first meeting, I meet Jenny, Mary and Sam and all talk excitedly about how they meet real people and deal with the problems of apartheid head on. They are passionate and full of life and hope. 'The work is hard but the personal rewards are great. We meet each month to catch up with each other, discuss the latest issues and support each other. We work in pairs in an office near the central station in the city and have the support of a wonderful Xhosa interpreter. He also speaks Zulu and several Tswansa languages. You'll love him. We all do.'

The Black Sashers work as advocates to people affected by apartheid laws. I remember how potent I felt standing in solidarity with other silent women showing the Apartheid government that we wouldn't let their barbarous policies proceed uncontested. I had felt at one accord with my political sisters, resolute and strong so I join their ranks and in this work I feel whole, passionate and free.

Now seven years after standing in protest at the University gates, we meet with people trapped in the never-ending labyrinth of red tape that ensures the privilege of employment is only for those deemed 'white'. In essence, a 'non white' person is caught in a perfect Catch 22. A black African can only apply for a residence permit in a particular area if they have full time employment, and only apply for work once they have a residence permit.

Apartheid has taken a long time to refine the policies that now constrain 'black people.'

In the 1970s more than three million souls are forcibly resettled in black 'homelands' created to rid South Africa of its Black citizens. These homelands are financially dependent, and most 'homeland citizens' become migrant labourers in South African cities and send money home to their families.

Once the Bantustans are in place, a 96-page document, called a reference book, expands the old Pass Law of 1952 to ensure government control over the movement of black Africans. African men and women who do not qualify to work in white urban areas have to carry a 'pass' that is valid for 72 hours. If they are caught with an expired pass, they are arrested and fined. If they have no money to pay the fine they are jailed for a few months. Little regard is given to how people are forced into poverty, family structure is destroyed or how large sections of the black population are criminalised.

At the Black Sash Advice Office, we work to try to understand the insanity of the laws entrenching 'white power' and find pathways through the morass to the illusive stamp on page three of the Black man's Pass. With this stamp the 'non white' soul can seek work.

I take up my new mission with great zeal, meet with other volunteers once a month to plan our process, and work once a week in the office as the ever-patient Des loves and nurtures my growing son and daughter. At Des's home, Richard has the company of her three older children and little Lisa has the devoted attention of both Des and her daughter Lindy. Richard becomes close friends with David, eighteen months his senior, a wonderful mentor in truth and mischief. With an outside interest, my sanity slowly returns.

***

A lady from our church joins the Black Sash and we often work together. Today we visit the Minister of internal affairs.

'Thank you Minister. We are happy to sit here and pray while you think about this problem.'

'Sorry ladies I've things to do'

'That's fine we won't disturb you. We'll pray quietly.'

The Minister for Internal Affairs sighs and picks up his phone.

'Marie can you bring these ladies a cup of tea please. Now if you don't mind I need to work. If you can pray outside please.'

'Certainly sir, but know that we'll be just outside your door talking to our Lord.'

We're ushered out, move a couple of chairs and settle in just outside the Minister's office. Marie brings us each a cup of tea.

When the Minister leaves the office an hour later, he sees us and smiles.

'Still here.'

'Yes sir, still praying.'

'Well I'll be out a while.'

'We'll be here on your return. Have a good lunch.' The Minister blushes.

He returns two hours later to find us still there.

'This is ridiculous. Don't you have things to do?'

'Nothing more important than this issue we have raised. It's impossible for the people who come to us. They need a home to get a Pass. They cannot get a Pass so they cannot get work. In their homelands, there are no jobs. Without a job, they cannot feed their children let alone afford a house. On your desk, we saw that quote "act justly and love mercy." You're a Christian and you want to do what God wills. Surely, He doesn't want people to starve. So we pray that you'll hear His voice and help us help the people who come for our assistance.'

'I see. Well I've work to do.'

The Minister walks past us into his office and shuts the door. We remain outside.

As we sit, heads bowed I consider our quiet protest. Without such brazen endeavors, nothing will change.

Just last week I spent four hours queuing with Thomas Mapedi waiting for the "white bass" who'd decide Thomas' eligibility for the stamp to be told to come back tomorrow because the queue was too long. Thomas was resigned. I was furious. He'd gone back the next day with another volunteer to be told that he first needed to queue in his "Bantustan". After several such incidents, we decided to protest and Ann and I volunteered for this job. When Khobe our "black interpreter" heard what we were doing he laughed.

'I hope your God will be listening. I cannot visit you in prison if you disappear.'

My response had been a chuckle, but inside I quaked. Now as I sit and wait all fear has gone. Someone has to hold these bastards accountable and I want to be among these.

The Minister's door opens and he stands before us.

'Well ladies it's almost time for your husbands to come home.'

He holds the door and ushers us back into his office. 'Sit please. I've decided you're right to help Thomas so I have written a letter to Mr. van der Merwe at the Pass office and asked him to help. I've not mentioned Thomas by name as you say there are many like him.'

'Thank you sir! God bless you. But sir, have you thought about the law itself?'

'The law is made by the parliament, not by me ladies; now be happy with what you have. Go home to your husbands.'

We stand say thanks and suggest we might be back. He sighs and we leave. We hit rush hour and are home late.

Thomas gets his stamp, the first step in an exhausting process of finding work. Hopefully he'll find employment before the police discover that he stays with a friend "illegally" because the government doesn't like unemployed black people staying in town.

Most Black Sashers are housewives home with young children. We have a phone tree and all celebrate our small win within hours. The news of our success travels quickly among users of the "Black People's Advice Office." Our queues increase. We work harder.

***

The pass laws are but one of many issues making the lives of non-whites unliveable and the response of those seeking to resist the Nationalist government's stranglehold is often protests. These become apparent to the complacent white population only when they reach big enough proportions to find their way onto the pages of our newspapers.

In 1976, thousands of black students walk from their schools to Orlando Stadium for a rally to protest against having to learn through Afrikaans in school. Police unsuccessfully attempt to calm the crowd and disperse the students using dogs and tear gas. When the students surround them, someone fires shots into the crowd and pandemonium breaks out.

More than 600 people are killed in Soweto, and unrest continues in the townships. Ongoing reports of turbulence stoke fear in the white population.

Politics take over

I don't drop the PFP but after the by-election politics slows. We've outgrown Mary's garage and buoyed by our success I offer our house as the office for the next election. Family life is immediately submerged in politics. We now live in a house converted from an old cinema with two separate living spaces. The smaller becomes the office, a hive of activity with bodies spilling out into the second, a lounge when we conduct meetings, stuff thousands of envelopes and chatter.

In the back yard we run a crèche under the tutelage of Sarah, a kindergarten teacher. When it grows and we hire a teenage helper to support Sarah. Now Richard and Lisa have friends, activity and can run to me when they want.

As our activities grow we become the talk of the neighborhood. One neighbour, an employee of the Bureau Of State Security (BOSS) visits Dave and me one Sunday. We invite him in, offer him coffee and a rusk, and he proceeds to ask us quietly about all the cars that are continually outside our fence. Dave talks openly about both the PFP and how wonderful it is to live in a democracy with rights to share our beliefs with others. Our neighbor talks about how interesting it is that both Afrikaners and Englishmen live in our suburb. I answer 'Yes, we are almost half and half now.' The chatter continues with us doing most of the answering of what seem friendly questions until I turn to our visitor and ask 'How's your new building working out?' When I worked, one of my tasks had been to estimate the number of parking places used for business within a block of our offices and I'd seen our neighbor going to his car in the new BOSS car park.

The tone of the visit immediately changed and was soon terminated by our flushed visitor. Soon after this, our letters from overseas are ripped open and resealed with sticky tape and our personal phone is tapped. I associate this with his visit.

During this time Steve Biko, a medical student, one of South Africa's most influential and radical Black Consciousness leaders, works to empower and mobilize the urban black population to resist apartheid. He is arrested and interrogated by security police and dies on September 12, 1977 at the age of

30, from brain damage sustained after a physical struggle with his interrogators, inadequate medical care and inhumane treatment.

Outrage about Biko's arrest, mistreatment and death sees him becomes a martyr of the Freedom Struggle. International interest in Biko's tragedy results in the strongest challenge yet to apartheid. The English press hound the then Minister of Police Jimmy Kruger about Biko's death. In response he speaks out at a National Party conference saying 'I am not glad and I am not sorry about Mr. Biko. It leaves me cold.' Biko's death and Kruger's response horrifies us and spurs us on to work even harder. We redouble our efforts, carefully prepare our brief and visit every household in our electorate three times. We will not be intimidated.

We stand a candidate against Kruger and choose a man with one of the most ubiquitous of Afrikaans names, van der Merwe. He is a gentle man who believes in our ideals but his name suggests to the electorate a God fearing Afrikaner who'll protect his country from the threat of the black man.

When we go to endorse him as adversary to Mr. Kruger we are kept waiting. Finally Minister Kruger enters the nomination room and as he strides past his stony gaze settles for a moment on me. 'I'll get you girly!' I shiver and my companions, both men, move closer.

We work solidly for months. For me this is more than a full time job because whenever any other volunteer is working, I'm obliged to be there. By Election Day we have seen every constituent household three times. We have elaborate plans for getting every voter to the polls. In South Africa there was no penalty for not voting, so keeping people involved and 'getting the voters out' was our biggest task.

The big day comes. We have a colourful marquee at every poling booth and workers rostered on throughout the day. There are those who mark off the voter's roll, those who keep tabs on which voters still have to come, people who offer coffee and cake, drivers and greeters. The other parties are astonished by our well-oiled machine, which ploughs on without let up. By the end of the day we are satisfied that every soul who promised to support us has voted. Now all that lies ahead is to scrutinize the counting and celebrate our efforts.

We're not supposed to know what's happening in the counting hall but hear a whisper that we have been getting all the votes in some pockets of the electorate. We see a Nationalist leaving the hall angry and begin to hope. By very early the next morning, it's clear the Nationalists have won government but we have engineered the biggest swing in the country. We are slightly disappointed heroes.

In the following weeks we wind up the office, thank our workers and finally take a holiday. An amazing chapter of my life ends.

A token white in Mr. Xhosa's black choir

Now I'm busy most days and don't think beyond family, church, the Advice office and the PFP, but I hear about a multiracial choir and decide to join. I have always loved to sing.

In the choir I'm challenged by very different relationships. In the normal South African world, 'blacks' step off the pavement, doff hats, and offer shuffling subservience and an obsequious 'Morning Missus.' Here there is no sign of the second-class citizen. We are welcomed openly and asked to contribute as equals.

Late every Tuesday evening Julie and I take the scary car ride into the no-mans-land of a 'coloured township' where we join a tolerant crowd of 'non-white' brothers and sisters who sing like angels and accept our meagre contribution to their wonderful harmony.

There's no piano so Mr. Xhoswe begins by banging his tuning fork against his bald head for our initial note. Sometimes we sing 'Nearer our God to Thee' and sometimes songs of resistance, which I don't understand but join with great gusto often to accompanying laughter and a hug from one of my companions. No questions, just a welcoming acceptance that we also sing for a free South Africa. When we sing Nkosi Sikeleli Africa, I drip with tears.

We practice for many months, setting aside tiredness from days begun at five to commute from homes in segregated Easterus into the 'white working world'. Finally, jovial, round faced Mr. Xhosa says we are ready to perform in Johannesburg. 'Make every endeavour to be there. An important "white man" will be listening to us.' Excitement abounds as we prepare to go. We stay back to sharpen renditions of the 'English songs'. We need to wow the mostly 'white audience' who won't understand most of what we sing.

Finally the day comes. I take jacket and handbag, arrived at my pick-up point early in the morning and wait for ages before the bus comes. As I climb aboard, I noticed baskets of food everywhere. I'm desolate. It hasn't struck me we'll need food; after all, it's only a bit over an hour to our destination. Everyone laughs as I stammer my apology.

'You don't yet know the Black way. You'll see.'

They're absolutely right. The trip before us is completely outside my experience.

For six hours, we start and stop along as people got on or off the bus, chat with people waiting to join us or have come to the bus just to say hi someone passing by. Each encounter is savoured. Catch ups include enquiries about the whole family and clan. While these progress others eat, drink, and communicate across the length of the bus. I haven't before been part of such a jubilant cacophony and while I understand few words this is clearly a celebration and all will extract every ounce of joy from this opportunity.

When the bus moves we sing in four or five part harmonies accompanied by peals of laughter. When we stop we talk, eat, chuckle or occasionally sigh. A woman cries and many gather round to comfort her. When we finally arrive at our destination, our hosts are quite put out. They've prepared a lunch now wilted and rehearsal time is short because we'll soon need to scrub up and go on stage. The women look well kempt and uniform in our white shirts and black knee length skirts and the men gay and glamorous in their white shirts bright red ties and beaming faces.

Our full-voiced four part harmonies fill the tattered old hall and rattle the doors, as people listen open mouthed from their rows of uncomfortable portable seats. In a couple of the African songs, 'black' voices from the segregated seats join our singing and it feels like the roof will blow off.

At the end of the performance the whites clap but the non-whites stand up and stamp their feet in appreciation. After a minute or two some whites join in. A pompous 'white' government representative condescendingly says how well we've done; the audience claps thunderously and asks for an encore. We sing again and the whole hall shudders with our excitement.

When the curtain, precariously strung up across the hall to separate stage from audience is drawn closed it collapses. We laugh uproariously, the whites slink out and our compatriots rush to join us in valuable congratulations. We have actually had the whities unknowingly clapping at our freedom songs.

I am incredibly sad that I'm going home with Dave and not the bus. When I planned I thought I'd be tired instead I'm elated and want more than anything to be with my choir. My day is over but the warmth and inclusiveness will remain with me as long as I live. What a ride. My small gesture of solidarity has given to me a glimpse of what it's like to wring joy from each moment. It's the zenith of my learning about community in South Africa.

I've now moved so far from the constraints of my family of origin that I fly. I feel alive and hopeful, have a new family in the church, choir and advice office, a wonderful understanding of solidarity with my black brothers and share in their lives. I begin to believe I can deal with Peter. If my community supports me, I can support my brother.

Outwardly, I'm now a different person. I speak out freely, celebrate being part of a vital opposition but sadly and more importantly, our circumstances have changed. A friend who works solidly for the Advice office disappears and within days, we know she is in prison because of her work. A short time later, I have a quiet visit from a friendly BOSS official, 'Do you want to bring up your children?'

I know exactly what he means and begin pushing Dave. 'We must leave South Africa.'

Else's death

Lisa is eighteen months and Richard almost three when I take a weekend to be with Mum. We are walking in the mountains when she sits abruptly struggling for breath.

Perhaps now's the time for that chat. There's so much to say before Mum dies, 'Mum do you ever think about death?'

'No why?'

'Because of your cancer Mum!! The doctor says you have secondaries. You know what that means, surely?'

'Don't ever talk about this again Jill. I'll fight this bastard and win so whatever you have to say will have to wait! Right now I need quiet to breathe and then we'll go on.' I sigh, perhaps with her fighting spirit she can overcome.

Dad, who's turned back, comes and takes Mum's arm. I don't want them to see my tears. Why did it take Mum getting ill for Dad to show any kindness?

This is one of the very few times we spend together without Peter, Dave or the kids and it's so peaceful. We're almost a normal loving family facing a difficult future together. But of course, this is foolishness. It's merely a reprieve. Tonight I'll go back home and they to Peter and tension will rise. I wish Mum could have a break.

***

A year later, our local church group sit in dappled shade below the spreading branches of a mulberry tree in our back garden. The sun is warm and children, perhaps a country dozen, shriek with laughter as they take turns sliding the full ten metres of a wet slip and slide. Replete after a shared meal, we now sip coffee over edifying conversation and watch with half an eye as the children play.

Into this lazy Sunday afternoon of communal Christian living comes the crashing reality of family.

Hans steers a shuffling Else towards us. We offer a chair and she sits bewildered. I speak and she answers, but her words make no sense. Hans turns to me, 'This may be her final visit to hospital. It's in her brain now.'

Over the following weeks my children spend their days and some nights with Des as I commute back and forward to Johannesburg and spend many hours with Else. It's hard to call this distorted, wracked entity Mum. The cancer has now metastasized and moved to her liver and brain. An enormous belly distorts her emaciated body and she looks grotesquely pregnant. The doctor explains, 'Her liver's riddled with cancer and it's growing exponentially.' Her mouth hangs open as she struggles to breath but each time she's given oxygen she wrenches the mask from her face. She's enormously agitated and in great pain. At first, I talk and Mum appears to understand what I am saying but doesn't reply. When she deteriorates, I sing to her.

Peter visits but Mum looks away, cries, and flays about as he approaches. He turns in anger, strides to the door, looks again and walks out. I get up, search up and down the corridor but he's gone, return go to cover Mum's toes and she gives me an almighty kick. Clearly, agitated by Peter she wants to let me know. My stomach is black and blue for a month after her death.

Next afternoon when Mum is restless, I sing 'Abide with Me.' She calms, looks directly into my eyes, smiles and slips into a peaceful coma. I spend most of each day and night at her bedside but Mum doesn't regain consciousness. When I ask her doctor he tells says she will die within hours. 'Nothing more we can do.' I sit and wait. Two days later Mum thrashes and pulls when two nurses thrust a tube down her throat. The doctor comes by says he will get a machine to keep Mum's heart beating. I look at him, 'If you put it on, I'll turn it off.'

He stops. Exhausted I decide to leave my endless vigil. Else, dies that night and we're called to the hospital to sign papers. A nurse asks if I wished to see her. I say no, scared to see her dead. I wish now that I had because my final memory is of Mum's face contorted by pain as she pulls at that damn tube from her throat. Dad, who saw her dead, says she was at peace.

As he speaks, I remember Mum's wiry dark hair and piercing blue eyes. She was a woman who pulled no punches. If she didn't like your dress, there was no quiet aside, her voice would resonate for all to hear, 'My God you look awful! You should never wear red!'

And again I see her now grey and leaning forward, her hands outstretched, bright blue eyes sparkling and mouth in a wonderful grin as she rocks the magnificent pine rocking-horse she gave Richard. He stands up and leans towards her as together they power the horse into furious action.

Mum was seldom at peace.

***

I spend the three days between Else's death and her burial at my old home. On the second morning, Hans comes into my room, 'Else came to visit me last night.'

I'm terrified. My father's hearing voices and seeing ghosts. Great! Mum is dead, Peter's a maniac and my dad has lost his grip on reality.

***

Funerals are expensive but there's a step-by-step guide, which makes organizing them easy. Suddenly it's important to Hans that Mum has a plain pine box Jews use but is cremated, a sacrilege. It's clear what music to choose, Mum loved Mozart. Dad asks in obituary notices that no one sends flowers, all tributes to cancer research.

I sit in the front of the crematorium with David. Richard and Lisa are with Des. The hall echoes with the deep full-throated resonance of Mozart's requiem but somehow this enlivens the electric energy of the mourners gathered to farewell Else. As the coffin is wheeled in people from both sides of the aisle step forward to place flowers on the box and mumble something before sitting again. The coffin is piled high with beautiful colorful flowers and Dad's wish is defied. His 'no fuss and don't waste money on flowers that go straight into the furnace' denied. I'm as overwhelmed by this bold denial as I am by the number of mourners who come to say goodbye. I choke with unspent emotion and drip with tears. I weep for the little girl whose Mum was the enemy offering no comfort, for the teenager whose Mum defended her in the face of a ravaging high school 'in crowd'. I cry for Mum so torn by racism and the trauma of fleeing Germany, only to watch another annihilation under Apartheid. I fight down the exhausting knowledge that the woman I finally grew to love and respect is gone forever. I cannot reconcile these extremities but let myself be with them. Dave squeezes my hand as Peter mumbles to himself and Dad wipes tears from his eyes. He looks angry. Perhaps he doesn't want to allow himself to grieve for Mum who he has known, taken responsibility for and fought with for so long.

Rex stands at the podium and begins.

'Elsa was a close friend from our first meeting when Hans and I returned from the North African campaign. She was a vital, energetic, outspoken and overpowering woman. Her forceful and uncompromising attitude to life left no one in doubt. Each of us knew where we stood with this vivacious, vibrant woman and no one will forget her tough pugilistic stance, her impeccable taste, her uncompromisingly modern handcrafted jewelry or those stunning animated blue eyes.

Else lived life large. Her love of the mountains comes first and is legendary. All of you who knew Else, as mountaineer will remember her pride at being in the party that first climbed the Bell in the Drakensburg. You will remember her endless restlessness, her magnificent contralto, her capacity to down mug after mug of sherry followed by her untamed use of four letter expletives, particularly around the campfire, and of course her insistence that swimming in cold mountain streams was only fun nude.

Else the silver-smith dressed in her dark blue workman's pants suit with insignia on pocket would make any prisoner proud. This uniform ensured her position as eccentric well-known artist throughout South Africa. Her love of paintings, music, theatre, books, tennis, good food, raucous company and political activism ensured she was never without company or idle. Else lived life out loud.

There is no point in pulling punches. Each of you will have witnessed some outrage, like Else tipping a treacle pudding over Hans' head. You would've heard her loud criticism of friends' taste in clothes, the government, the way a man treated his wife, the fact that Margo, Mary or Mable allowed her husband to use her as a doormat. I see your smiles. Which one of you did not think of ducking for cover at one stage or another?

However, we're all here to honour Else. She was a remarkable woman. Each of us overflows with memories of her vitality, joy, anger and determination to do everything exactly the way she wanted despite any attempts to tame her. It was good knowing you Else and all our lives have been enriched by knowing you.' The hall reverberates with recognition.

Words spoken and farewell given, the crowd rises noisily to leave. As they exit, they hug me in condolence. I recognize the many disparate groups with whom Mum was involved. To my utter surprise, there are also several friends of mine who say they will never forget Else's irresistible character and outspoken ways.

I am deeply moved and find it difficult to leave the crowd of mourners to go and prepare for those who will join us at home. I would've liked to sit alone a while and farewell my mother in silence.

Back to the realities of life

Within a week of Else's death, Hans introduces me to his lover. 'Brigitte and I have known each other for a couple of years. She kept me sane through Else's illness.' I'm stunned, angry and speechless and instantly resent her. How could she and Dad expect me to accept her so soon after Mum's death? When I tell David he hugs me. I see shock in Des's eyes and her uncharacteristic lack of words.

Within five weeks, they marry. Dad sells our house, forces Louisa and Tom into retirement and beds down Peter's residence in a Tara outpatients halfway house. The newly-weds now move to the farm that Hans had bought for his and my mother's retirement.

I'm furious about the affair, that Mum has been so unceremoniously usurped, that I have had no time to mourn and that Brigitte expects acceptance and even gratitude that she has looked after Dad through Mum's illness. Couldn't he have waited a decent mourning period? Brigitte is German, drives a BMW when Dad has always sworn 'I'll never accept the willful acquiescence of Germans to Hitler's rule. I hold them accountable, every one.'

As this imposter moves into my childhood home, packs up Mum's household and begins laughing at her possessions. I'm outraged but say nothing, scared I will not be able to contain my anger and humiliation. 'What is this?' Brigitte holds up a precious azure blue milk jug from Mum's trousseaux. There's a small chip in the spout. 'Did your mother have no pride? I will have to take things in hand. If your parents had been struggling, I'd understand but your father always provided well.'

Not a good start. When we visit the farm at Christmas and I see dahlias, Mum's pet hate, in her favorite Bosch vase I can hold my tongue no longer. 'How dare you put those putrid flowers in Mum's vase?' Brigitte gives me the vase and I throw the flowers in the outside bin. Neither of us speaks about it again and when I leave, I take the vase with me.

Hans is executor of Mum's will and Peter and I the beneficiaries. In this capacity, he decides not just how but also what possessions and assets he'll split. Else owned little, a Mini, a workshop full of jeweller's tools, some jewellery made for sale in her shop, a few art works and a small amount of 'special' money she had earned and set aside.

I want her tools because they're so much part of Mum, and David would like to try making jewelry, but we have no place for them. Hans sees the art as his, despite Else's clear ownership, so excludes these. I ask for the Mini saying I'll pay Peter half but Hans says it's not fair, as Peter cannot drive. I don't understand his logic but know it's pointless to argue. Peter's share of the estate goes into his trust 'which exists to protect you and help once I'm gone and you're left to watch over Peter.' I never question Hans' decisions because arguing with Dad about taking anything from Peter, even with Peter's agreement and recompense is pointless. Dad's view is immutable. In the end, I am allocated some jewellery and a little cash. I buy three duvets because I hate bed-making with sheets and blankets. The rest, a small amount of money but our first unallocated resource, goes into the bank.

***

With Mum buried, Peter in his halfway house and Dad at the farm, I continue to immerse myself in community life. My PFP work has slowed, I have spare time and notice I'm unable to truly hear those who come into the Advice Office. I ask around and am told that I can learn more about listening by becoming a Life Line volunteer. I phone, am selected and begin my training. I practice listening skills on everyone and am astounded when Richard responds to my listening and begins to chatter openly.

I begin to build deeper relationships basically by keeping quiet and making sure I understand what I hear.

There are many exhausting calls at Life Line and callers often trigger personal issues. With each interaction, I learn about myself and to my surprise find that many of my issues are ordinary.

Very quickly, working at Life Line becomes political. I answer a call from a young woman phoning from a phone booth in the early stages of labour. She is homeless and has nowhere to give birth. I spend several hours trying to locate somewhere for her to have her child. Finally a convent agrees to take Sarah in if I find somewhere for her to move once she and the baby are ready. Desperate I agree, search but find nothing, so having given my word decide to take Sarah into our own home.

Within hours my church pals find everything I need to support a mum and baby and a week later Sarah moves in. Helping at arms length is easy but living with and supporting a stranger with very different attitudes to life is difficult.

I arrive home from shopping and David is sitting at the dining room table arms crossed. 'Jill, this time you've gone too far!'

'What's happened?'

'I was lying in bed reading the paper when Sarah came in and offered to pay me for taking her into our home in kind.'

'What's that mean?'

'She said she is used to pleasing men and likes having half white babies.'

'She what?'

'Said she's used to paying her own way, became quite distressed when I wasn't interested. Sorry Jill, she needs to go now!'

I move heaven and earth and finally find help and my activities become more circumspect.

I don't have a 'non-white' person living in my home but each time I see my BOSS neighbour, and he smiles and asks me how my family's doing, my stomach tightens as I remember a similar smile from his associate.

I keep on at David that I want to leave South Africa and after several months of nagging David agrees to take the money Mum left us and buy a ticket to Australia to find a job. At first, he finds nothing but within three weeks, he travels to Melbourne, looks for work within his field and is interviewed by a man who has read one of David's recent publications. He is offered a job and the organization is willing to pay for our resettlement expenses. As soon as Dave lets me know he has found work, I sell the house and start packing.

We stay with Des and Mike for the final five weeks before we emigrated. This time is wonderful.

My coming to Pretoria ten years before was quiet and unassuming, overwhelmed by my uncontrollable struggle to be with people. Our leaving is anything but. Every evening is filled with goodbyes. I am astonished there are so many people sad to see us go.

Elaine, a staunch PFP and Black Sash comrade, lives in a huge contemporary ranch style dwelling in the country. French doors spill out onto a patio covered in Bougainvillea and down to lush green lawns and a magnificent pool, perfect for parties. Beyond the pool the lawn blends into the South African Savanna where Impala wander under flat-topped Acacia trees. Here we are the guests of honour at a farewell of a lifetime.

She and others prepare for days, filling her beautiful place with bunting, flowers, food and bubbly. Friends from a well-known township band play until dawn. Well over a hundred and fifty souls join us in a riotous night of celebration and solace. Several make speeches loud, long and filled with laughter, remembrance and regret. People Dave knew as servile 'black' work mates come and shake our hands, look us in directly in the eye and wish us well. White compatriots say they will miss us but give us missions to share their plight with the world. We leave at four in the morning, exhausted. The next day we leave for Australia.

As Des and Mike wave us off Des says with tears running down her cheeks 'You may as well be going to Mars.' Her son David who is eight years old and Richard's best mate, kicks the tires of the car as we leave in Chris' microbus and won't say goodbye. Des tells me later that he was upset for several days and difficult to manage. Only later did she realize that this was his way of expressing his grief at losing a close friend.

Once at the airport Chris helps us with our numerous cases, entertains the kids as we book in and comes with us to the gate. Here we say goodbye and I reluctantly let go of Chris' hand. She smiles at me and says 'Thank you Jill, you have taught me a great deal about kindness. Go with God.'

For most of the flight to Australia, on an airplane filled with emigrants, my young son talks to his reflection in the window pretending it is David. 'He says that when we get to Australia I must run away, go back to Africa and live with him.' I swallow my tears and wonder what I've done to my family. It's because of me that we are leaving. If I had not been so insistently against the status quo I could've escaped the fear of going to prison as a couple of compatriots had, and there would be no need to leave Africa for Australia and start again.

RECOVERY

Australia

We all arrive jetlagged and tired but Dave insists that we drop our belongings at the hotel, head for the harbor and make the most of our three days in Sydney before heading to Melbourne where David has secured a job.

He strides ahead and jumps onto a roaring red rattler as it pulls into Central station. People rush everywhere. The wind from the trains as they sweep in, grind to a stop and speed off takes my breath away, and the cacophony of voices, shrieking trains and a ferry tooting in the background all remind me of my utter alienation in this big bustling city twelve thousand kilometres away from home.

David wants us all to take this opportunity to experience the treasures of this beautiful city, but as I hold on to little Lisa with one hand and her tugging, inquisitive brother Richard with the other, terrified of becoming separated from them or Dave, I cannot share his enthusiasm. He has all money and passports, and knows where he is going having spent two weeks here looking for work. I wish I could say that I enjoyed those days but they are all a blur. The crowded city is filled with the cacophony of chaotic traffic, the harbor big, blue and bustling with boats of every size and shape, the weather hot and humid, and I drip with sweat. Jetlagged and stressed, I just want to return to the hotel and sleep. But when we finally do return to the very basic motel on the busy Pacific Highway through Chatswood, I am so wired that I can't rest. I quake at the stage-set impermanence of this city. Our room reverberates with the rumble of traffic just outside our door. The light coruscates across the railway line in bright unforgiving flashes and a million twinkling lights disturb the darkness. So instead, I sit up watching an unintelligible television chat show, and am again assaulted by strange accents and the fully saturated, gaudy color of a picture my exhausted mind cannot process, while the rest of my family slumbers.

In Melbourne, we are settled into a hotel close to the city and on a tram route to David's new work place. He immediately starts at ICI and the kids and I are taken firmly in hand by a settlement consultant who supports the families of newly arrived workers for the first six months. I am astounded by ICI's generosity and care. This young woman knows Melbourne well and helps us find temporary accommodation close to good public schooling and within driving distance of David's work. I don't like the newer suburbs she initially suggests, because they are far from the city and David's work. These large but insubstantial brick veneer 'McDonald' style houses on small blocks of land with no trees or gardens are far from public transport and shopping facilities and we will only have one car. When I raise these concerns I am shown a semi-detached house in what I later find out is a wealthy established older suburb just across the river from the city in leafy Kew. Here there are trees, shops, a tram and a good local school within easy walking distance.

The following week we move in and I immediately find the nearest school, Kew Primary, with the intention of enrolling Richard. I dress both children in their new yellow rain coats, hats and galoshes and we walk the five rain-soaked, leafy blocks. As we approach the traditional red brick schoolhouse, an exact replica of Richard's old school I smile. Richard runs through the gate and up a concrete pathway to the office in exactly the same place it had been in his previous school. He is eager to begin his new school life. Lisa, who is almost invisible beneath her rain gear, holds my hand and skips happily beside me as we follow. We are greeted by the neatly-dressed matronly head mistress, Ms Smith who welcomes us to Australia, enrolls Richard and then turns to me. 'How old is the beautiful young lady?'

'Lisa turned five just last Thursday.'

'Well then Lisa, you are old enough to begin school too. Would you like that?'

She beams 'Yes please.'

I gulp, not ready to begin my life without daytime company but not brave enough to argue my case. Unwilling to undercut their excitement I agree that both start school immediately and walk them each along the raised wooden duckboard pathways strung across soggy lawns to their portable classrooms. The headmistress turns to me 'Perhaps you should say goodbye here. The canteen will supply Richard and Lisa with free lunch for their first day. You can fetch them at three.'

'Oh, OK then.'

'They will be fine for today. Lisa, Richard, kiss Mum goodbye. She can meet your teachers when she fetches you. I don't want to disrupt classes now.' Both kids peck me on the cheek and wave goodbye as Ms Smith takes each by the hand. I turn away and head for home, plonk myself in front of the telly and wonder what I will do until 3:00.

***

That night, and three months of nights to follow, I wake in the silence of the death hour. Alienation clings to the syrupy heat of the night as I fight my way out of a dream replete with images of community and country. My community. My country, in South Africa, my home. In Melbourne, I am an alien. Nothing is familiar, not even the grey misty sky; a poor replacement for the infinite blue skies of home.

The lack of clear purpose with no sense of belonging or friendship or place overwhelms me. I have no stake in this new world. I wait for someone to know me so that life can begin.

It rains continually from when we arrived in June until November. In Pretoria, I would retire to bed on any overcast day. Here I fight the desire to stay in bed, pull the blankets over my head and hibernate. It rains and it rains and it rains. We wake to foggy mornings and retire at night under a soggy grey sky with no sign of stars. Dave works, the children have school and I, the do-gooder South African housewife, fights the depression that descends and cloys like these dank dark mists of winter. Writing helps so I pen letters filled with bittersweet sadness and longings for home.

I listen to the news but 'bread and butter' politics has no meaning after the horror of Apartheid. I get it that Labor 'left' supports 'the battler' and that the Liberal 'right' supports 'free enterprise and having a go' but nobody here seems surprised by the massive 'safety net' that supports all Australians. The gentleness of this politic, so solidly wedded to democracy and parliamentary debate is unfathomable. That government works at prioritizing its promises to its electorate is almost too good to be true. But where do I stand? In South Africa, it was all so clear. There was right and wrong. It was black and white so to speak.

I have become addicted to the politics of life and death and to testing myself against this measure. Without it, I fight to feel alive. Is this what it means to be a foreigner and if so how will I ever fit in?

My first encounter with Social Security is when I register for a parents' allowance. Helping others negotiate the Apartheid system in the Black People's Advice Office in South Africa I had felt angry, scorned, and resolute. But this bureaucracy! How patronizing. The building is utilitarian, the industrial, scuff marked, grey carpet will last forever and the rows of chairs in the waiting area are a moldering mustard. I stand in an endless queue, get to the front swap my name for a number and am told to sit until called. Many disconsolate souls wait without expectation for their turn to come up. Have they nothing to do or nowhere to be. They simply sit and wait while my insides scream. 'How long before I become like them? Get on with it.'

When finally called, I walk up to the glass-fronted counter, look the administrator in the face and say what I need. She looks at her computer screen and mumbles

'How long 'ave yer been in Melbin and wha's yer 'dress.'

'Excuse me I'm not sure what you said. Could you please slow down.'

'Ne're mind. D'yer have yer own bank account?'

'We have just opened a joint account. Like we had in South Africa,'

'You will need an account of yer own. In Australia yer a person in yer own right and should 'ave the freedom te bank separately.'

I argue, 'I don't want freedom. Dave and I work together as a couple.'

'The law 'ere is that yer have to bank separately to get any government payment.'

'But . . . This is my decision.'

'Sorry. There's no but.'

I open a bank account and go back. Another charming but condescending worker says, 'Congratulation you are now free to spend the money on your children, as you see fit.'

Some choice.

My first encounter with 'socialism' leaves me skeptical. 'Is this a gentle form of social control and if so, does it render people powerless?'

I write to Dad.

'Dear Dad, I know you warned me that settling in a new country would be difficult but I did not know what you meant till now.

Relating to people is hard. Everyone is very polite and friendly and very willing to help me understand my new country but their expectations are so high. They want so badly to hear that Australia is wonderful and all I see is how different and disappointing life is. The sky is grey and the misty rain seems to soak into my brain, a murky muddle of immovable sorrow. I cannot shake my extraordinary longing to be among the people I know and I would do anything to see and hear a single black soul.

The canteen at the kid's school where I volunteer and the streets and supermarkets are filled with chirpy white women talking about fashion, the latest recipe, the best coffee or a drink spot. If it's not footy it's cricket, the tennis, going to the gym and then of course the endless discussion of all the activities their children do. I understand this is the gossip of acquaintances and know that it will take time to make friends but I find myself tongue-tied and at a loss when engaged in issues of no consequence. Who would have guessed that weather and everyday conversation are so important?

But let me shake free of this malaise and talk about what is real. Both Richard and Lisa love school and feel at home in their vibrant, fun-filled classrooms. Children's artwork is everywhere; Richard and Lisa love 'Show and tell' where each child gets a chance and as for reading and arithmetic they are taught in a completely different way.

David loves work and travels there by train, an hour each way from Kew but this leaves me with the flexibility to shop for food and to begin looking for a permanent home in the little Holden

Gemini. Perhaps once we have our own place I will settle. I must find something meaningful to do.

Dad, is this the sort of thing you found difficult when you first arrived in South Africa or were your issues different? For you there was language, no work and a myriad of other obstacles and I feel ashamed talking about my struggle in the light of these but I must talk to someone.

I can't tell Dave that I struggle to rise and get the kids to school or that I often come home and sit disconsolately in front of the television trying to understand my new world. I know I left hoping for a gentler life where politics with a capitol P did not colour all and now I find the endless discussion of interest rates, unions and the global oil price boring. I find socialism patronizing and have a sneaking suspicion that supporting those in most need encourages dependence and contributes to learned helplessness. One program I watched discussed that patterns of dependency are now being seen in the second generation of people getting security benefits from the government. I miss so many of the things I found overwhelming and realize that, as I grappled with the excruciating politics of exclusion, I found significance. How 'sick' is that.

Now my struggle is with feelings of anxiety about my utter alienation.

Sorry Dad I shouldn't dump on you when you have so many concerns back home.

How are Mandy and Peter getting along and where did they meet? Have you seen them lately and how is Brigitte?

Please write soon. I miss you and am sure you can help me find some perspective.

Love Jill'

His response to my letter is short and to the point.

Jill,

You chose to get into politics in South Africa and are now managing the inevitable consequences. I warned you not to run an election campaign from your home. I also told you that moving countries is difficult. Remember why you left. You cornered yourself and leaving became your only safe alternative. So, get on with it. You will settle in time.

Peter and Mandy the meshuggeneh are now settled in a flat in Hillbrow with three cats that stink the place out. They have much in common and keep themselves occupied with their mutual illnesses, pills and outpatients at Tara. Peter is fine and sticks to his doctor's instructions at present but he will never work. He and Mandy will come to the farm for Christmas and Mandy's daughter will look after their cats.

My experiences were different from yours and I was happy to be offered a refuge in a strange new land.

Now get on with your life and remember that one day Peter will become your responsibility.

Dad.

I read this letter but feel no better.

Dave has work and the children have school but I have no anchor in this new land. We search for and purchase a property and I become more settled. We buy a cat and her kitten to make our house home and I apply to join Lifeline as a volunteer counsellor, my first investment in a personal future.

The fire

We have been in Australia for three months and in our new house for a month. The kids are at school and I am cleaning up after breakfast. I hear footsteps and look up as Dave walks into the kitchen. His face is grey. 'What's up, why are you home it's only eleven?'

'There was a fire at work. My lab is gone. The whole wing burned. When I got there, smoke was billowing out of the building and fire trucks were everywhere. People were just standing outside the fence gaping. Then some people tried push past the firemen to go into the buildings, so they sent us all home.'

Next morning, Duncan a colleague who arrived in Australia two weeks before us comes to talk to David. They sit huddled together in two canvas chairs beside the French doors leading out onto the back lawn. David looks ravaged, glasses off and rubbing his eyes as Duncan leans close and quietly questions and coaxes him. After he leaves, Dave tells me 'Duncan tried to persuade me to sign a statement saying the fire started in my fume cupboard.'

'What?'

'He asked me to sign a statement saying that the fire started not only in my fume cupboard but also that it was my equipment that caught fire.'

'What did you do?' I am terrified. We have risked our whole future in coming here, have mortgaged ourselves to the hilt with just enough left over to live and save towards buying furniture, household goods and all the other things that make for a comfortable new life. Is this the end of that dream? I bite my tongue. Say nothing, try to still the cacophony in my head. David is struggling and I must support him, not force him to hide his feelings for my sake.

I try to hide my panic the next morning as we drive off to buy a couple of power tools so that David can build us each a wooden bed base for the mattresses that now sit on the floor. I must show confidence in Dave but my fear is almost overwhelming. I can feel my old responses fighting for supremacy. My insides scream 'Stop! Don't spend. You'll lose your job and never get another. We can't waste a cent. Let's hunker down and hide. - Don't pretend - there's no future.'

We get the tools and order timber to make the kids' beds and I remain silent. Well, I don't speak but I'm sure Dave, who says nothing, knows my fears.

A week later, I am booked into a Life Line training weekend and go reluctantly, to show Dave I trust him to cope without me, despite the fire.

I will never forget the scene that awaits me on my return. At the door stands David, holding Lisa's hand and she in turn holds Richard's. All three faces are down cast and sombre. As I walk in Lisa looks up at me tears brimming and says, 'My kitty is dead Mummy. Daddy drowned Smokey in the dishwasher.'

All of us walk through the kitchen and into the family room with its two canvas chairs, sit on the carpet and cry. The last week has been difficult for all of us.

Our lovely little kitten, with his grey fur and chocolate box green eyes is dead, as are our dreams for his future. Gorgeous, inquisitive, bouncy Smokey with his super soft pelt and his mum with her gentle ginger and grey stripes are a replacement for our two cats and a dog left behind with friends, despite us all loving them dearly. Three months in quarantine was too cruel to contemplate. We miss their company. Alexis, Russell and Heidi were part of our family.

That night we all cling together on the mattress in our bedroom with only a sheet and an inadequate blanket as cover. Mum cat mews for her baby outside our room as we finally fall asleep. She is at our feet when we wake the next morning. David is still away from work so we skip school for the day to bury Smokey.

We have a solemn service. David digs a small grave under the towering lemon scented gums in our back yard, Lisa sings 'Jesus loves me' and Richard throws the first sod onto the small box containing our beloved kitten. Again, we weep and then finally leave the small grave and go in to breakfast. Mum cat does not accompany us, she sits outside beside the freshly turned earth and we all know she needs to be alone with her pain. Later that day Lisa draws a picture of Smokey and puts it on the wall next to her bed. 'At least,' I console myself, 'we have each other.'

***

For a couple of weeks before the fire there had been a train strike, so Dave had car-pooled with a couple of others traveling to work before rush hour and leaving early. On the night of the fire, he had gone before his lab mates leaving a safe experiment running in the left hand section of the fume cupboard overnight. Others not affected by the train strike had worked back.

In the week after the fire, David returns to work and is asked to go back into his lab and do an inventory of what was destroyed in the fire. Duncan, David's senior, is put in charge of documentation for their laboratory. David's concern about Duncan's behavior grows.

'Duncan is being strange and I found Adrian going through the ashes in the fume cupboard behind the police tape today. Something is going on. It's fishy!'

When David hears rumors that Duncan pushed past the firemen to his office and the lab and took photographs on the morning after the fire he is convinced something is wrong. Then one morning Dennis the lab technician says 'If I am asked what happened, you might be surprised by what I say.' David feels an unspoken expectation to accept responsibility for the fire that he knows he has not instigated.

He now searches through the ashes himself and finds his equipment in the left section of the fume cupboard collapsed in the ashes where the wooden bench burned out beneath it. In the centre of the fume cupboard is a pile of white ash indicating that this is the seat of the fire.

Dave is exhausted. He does not know what to do. Finally one night he comes home and says 'I have asked for a full forensic enquiry into where the fire started.' Some time later a report completely exonerates him.

Weeks later Dave tells me 'I was called into a meeting with Duncan today and I was asked what experiments he had been doing.'

'And?'

'Well Duncan? said he couldn't remember so I was asked to help reconstruct what experiments he had been doing.'

'What did you say?'

'Well I was pretty sure that he had set up an experiment in the fume cupboard after I left work on the evening before the fire so I began to piece things together.'

'And what about Duncan?'

'Well he continued saying he couldn't remember.'

The following week Duncan is fired but he threatens to call in his union. He is reinstated and David is expected to continue working with him.

This is not the end of the story because despite David's exoneration the shadowy stigma that he started the fire and should just have taken responsibility for it remains for many years. I cannot shake the fear that my protector is lamed and begin to worry that we are not welcome in Australia. Our daily life continues but in the depth of the night, my fear returns. I jump at my silhouette in the mirror. Strange things lurk in the cupboard and as the wind whispers through the trees, I freeze in fright.

He skulks in the shadows, relentless and wild

in his search for a tender, delectable child.

With his steely sharp claws and his slavering jaws

oh he's waiting . . . just waiting . . . to get me.

***

We find a church very different from our close community of believers in South Africa but they organize small groups who meet once a week in the home of a group leader. Here we share a meal, talk about our lives, study the bible and pray together, about ourselves, Australia and the world beyond. These people are caring and genuine, and slowly I begin to trust and become involved in their lives. We become foster carers and for the next few years we offer emergency care and then take on a teenage girl who stays for fifteen months before returning to her family. My involvement in Life Line and the new community settles me, I start investing in new friendships and my letters to South Africa become less frequent.

At Life Line, I learn that there are Australians who respect, listen, are generous with and interested in people outside their immediate community. On the other hand, I hear that, as in South Africa, family violence and sexual assault are ubiquitous, that drugs and alcohol are a big problem and that homosexuality is beginning to be discussed openly. Suicide is the issue we spend most time discussing, as an immediate, calm response is always important.

I remember clearly my first suicidal call. A young woman recently raped was too ashamed to talk to her parents. She phoned having taken a full bottle of aspirin. My heart raced but, as taught, I forcibly slowed my breathing and talked quietly into the phone, beckoned for help myself because I was in training, asked how many pills and got an address and permission to call an ambulance. Exhausting! Towards the end of the call, the voice at the other end of the line became slurred. My heart leapt and my trainer patted my hand. I looked at her and tried to slow my breathing again.

I remember the incredible visceral tingling relief at hearing an ambulance siren getting closer. The knock on the door and calming voice saying 'We have her now' was wonderful. I burst into tears.

At Lifeline I find a friend who seems to understand me. Sanchita an Indian woman has spent some time in Zimbabwe. When I talk to her about feeling like I'm from Mars she laughs, 'It takes anyone who comes from Africa a couple of years to get over their paranoia! People who have not lived with Apartheid, which is as bad in Zim, will just not understand how you are always looking over your shoulder.'

Sanchita is a Godsend, she and I travel together to Lifeline and take the same shifts. We meet once a week for a coffee at either her house or mine and I am delighted to see pictures on her wall and vibrant colors in her home. We laugh together about the Australian bland, discuss books and movies and of course our kids. Sometimes we talk about being separated from family. One day I talk about leaving Peter. It is strange to invite someone from my new country into my shadowy past. Is it a mistake? I so want to escape the burden of Peter and his illness.

Looking back at the Boogieman

Life Line has become second nature and I am now a trainer. We, the volunteer backbone of the organization, work alongside staff to recruit, plot, plan and run all training for telephone counsellors and I love my involvement. Somehow, I have an innate ability. I am a natural.

This autumn weekend the trainers and our leader J head for the hills. We wind our way up tarred roads, along misty silent lanes, through a broad stone gateway and park beneath shedding beach trees. We dump our belongings in freestanding stone cabins and head for the central conference room where we huddle around a big open fireplace, chat and sip cocoa before sitting together in a broad inclusive circle to begin our work together.

We start gently. Each of us is given a persona who will tell our story of coming away from our busy lives. Then we refocus on our hopes for the weekend. I am a bright brand new pink toothbrush bought especially for this trip away. My job is to describe what it has been like to be packed together with personal items in Jill's sponge bag, to be released from the bag zipped tight for the journey up into the hills and placed together with a new tube of Colgate toothpaste in a glass awaiting Jill's return to her cabin. What did I experience on the way up to Booth House. What was it like to be shoved away in the dark, to be released to sit with Jill's expectations for this weekend? Am I aware of her feelings in the car as we drove up? What did I see, hear, touch, smell or taste? Once I am fully immersed in my role as others are in theirs it is our job to interact. We have a wonderful evening filled with observations, stories, insights and laughter. As a bright pink toothbrush I am able to say things that the retiring Jill may not have and I get to know the hat, posh striped leather handbag and an umbrella in a way that I may not have learned about John or Mary or Mather. Before we leave our gathering for the night J asks us to consider 'What does your persona have to say about your family history and can this teach you something new about your role as telephone counsellor and trainer?'

I stroll down the path with Dorothy and turn aside to my secluded cabin. I am effusive.

'What an evening! Good night, sweet dreams.'

I hum as I enter my quiet cabin, shower, take up my battered old green toothbrush cover it in toothpaste and smile 'dowdy old thing you need replacing.'

It's quite chilly so I jump into bed pull up the covers and snuggle in. There is a bedside clock. It's eleven. 'On my own with nothing until breakfast at eight what a luxury.'

***

Awake I stand shivering beside my bed. It's one thirty. The wind howls outside and rain clatters on the tin roof. My heart is in my mouth and I can hardly breath. I look around. Where am I, what is that shuffling sound, who is here, where is he, how the hell do I protect myself and what is that scream?

I force myself to sit on the bed and begin talking to myself. 'Slow down! Breathe! Get into bed and turn on the light.' I do. Now floods of tears overwhelm me. 'Where is the Boogieman?' I look, and then stop as I remember my dream. We were in the mountains Mum, Dad, Peter and me and Peter has a brick sized rock raised above my head. I want to run but my feet won't carry me . . . and then I wake.

For the rest of the night I huddle under the covers. By morning, I feel incoherent and inconsolable. I have remembered my family and I am scared shitless. I do not want to be here.

I shuffle in to breakfast unable to speak. Others chatter and invite me into conversation but I decline saying I have a headache. Later as we gather to begin our work, I sit mute tears running down my face. People ask what's wrong but I can't speak. The more people ask the further I retreat. Someone offers to chat to me outside, another to take me home but I shake my head, walk out and wander the grounds sobbing. I miss lunch for fear of having to speak. I go to my room and try to refocus, then give up, take three headache pills and go to bed. I sleep until morning.

The next day I have stopped crying but am still mute. I can't get my head together. All I see and hear is my inside screaming. I sit in the group but my soul will not settle. I am there but not. My mind has gone walkabout. I cannot relate to either the people or my surroundings. I am an automaton, much like Peter after IST. I just cannot get myself together.

By the time Dorothy drops me home at the end of the weekend we are all convinced that I am mad. As the car stops outside my home, I grab my bag and rush inside where I run into the bathroom and hide behind the toilet. A couple of hours later Dave, who has tried to find out what happened, drags me out from my hideout and he and the kids put me to bed and sit with me as I sob myself to sleep. When I wake the next morning, I am disoriented and desolate but able to engage in household tasks. A couple of days later I am back to myself.

***

I have the devil of a time convincing my Life Line trainer that I have had a flash back, but that I am again functional. Reluctantly she gives me a second chance.

'But Jill we will be watching you closely.'

'Fair enough. Me too.'

***

At Life Line, I learn that most mothers work when their children are at school and they can do with some extra cash. Volunteer work isn't considered work, so I take the suggestion of a fellow Lifeliner and look for a paid position at Social Security, the Fraser government's Centrelink.

I find an advert for a job at a local council. Remembering that David found work by going in person, I copy the details down and head off to say 'good-day.'

The Nunawading city offices are in a low sleek building set away from the main road on beautiful green lawns. When I enter and ask for the town planning department I am ushered into a light filled waiting room looking across the lawns to a sophisticated purpose built playground. This is so civilized. When the guy I have asked to meet strides out hand extended I become very shy. He immediately puts me at ease by asking me where I am from. 'It sounds like New Zealand or South Africa from your accent.' I blush. When he hears that I have come to enquire about the town planning job he becomes more dismissive. 'We only take applications in writing. If you need to know more about

158

the position you can get a position description at the front desk.' Now I am embarrassed, say a quick 'thank you' and turn to hide my burning cheeks. When I do put in a formal application, I am told that while my experience is relevant, my qualifications are not recognized in Australia and without them, I will not find work in town planning.

We need to stretch our family income so I find temporary work as a market researcher but am useless because I listen rather than filling out forms. My bosses say they can only pay me per interview and because I am so slow, I earn very little.

When I speak about my problem at a Life Line training session several months into my work on the phones, a trainer smiles and suggests I go back to study psychology. 'Studying is now free and accessible to all,' she tells me.

'What do you mean?'

'Australian universities used to cost a fortune. But then we had a PM called Gough Whitlam who made them free. He also stopped us fighting in Vietnam, demanded equal pay for women, abolished university fees, established Medibank and extended benefits for single mothers among one or two other important things that have changed the shape of Australia.'

'Fantastic. Socialism really rocks. What happened to Gough?'

'What happened to Gough? Well that might take a while but he was dismissed as Prime Minister by the Governor General; Fraser was put in as caretaker Prime Minister who then called for a double dissolution election, and won.'

'Sounds like a wild ride. And here I was thinking Australian politics are boring.'

She smiles. 'Have fun with your studies.'

I make the decision to attend Swinburne University, easily accessed by public transport and with a good reputation for Psychology. Sancheta helps with the forms and soon I am registered as a student.

My trainer friend is right. University is free, my life is firmly back on track, studying Psychology will help me gain insight into my family of origin, recover from fears that I am stupid and prepare me for the Australian workforce.

Despite past fears I find that studying psychology is easy because most of it happens in the head and not in the heart. It's easy to think about feelings, schemas, psychological conditions, issues, and social psychology. It is living that is difficult. So, for years, I study, write essays and talk about the ins and outs of people, groups and societies, and dysfunction, and finally in my fourth year I begin to sit opposite another soul and listen.

Perhaps the best part of studying is that it fits so well with the family. I study while the children are at school and in the evenings, we sit together and do homework. David joins us, reads or dozes in front of the fire or the TV.

My next step towards becoming a psychologist is a placement in the community and I choose an organization that will allow me to work with couples and families because I want to be able to work from a systemic approach that helps all family members. This is particularly important, as I always felt excluded from issues with Peter, which affected my life.

To all intents and purposes, we are now settled, but there are still moments, usually when I am alone, that I think back to the easy friendships and deep understanding I had with people who know my history – when I, Des and other church women sat together chatting about our children under clear blue skies, drinking tea and eating delicious, oven dried sourdough rusks not found in Australia. Or the camaraderie of animated political discussions as I worked with other to bring about change. The deep emotional connection with country, community and kin is missing in new relationships. I am here, an Australian; I love my new country but sometimes still feel a hollowness. I am so different. An outsider. I miss South Africa's earthiness, its color and cultural connection, and the grittiness and angst of my family. In truth after Mum's death, the connections with Dad and Peter became brittle. Despite this, my soul belongs to Africa and I feel responsible for both Dad and Peter, I cannot let them go.

Hans Appears

Until now, I have not truly known Hans the man, only Dad my father. In gaining some understanding of him, I begin to know myself, my relationship with my family and am able to gain some perspective on my connection with Peter.

***

I go to answer our front door wondering who is knocking at just after six in the morning and there before me is Hans with Brigitte two steps behind. 'Well can I come in?' I stand flabbergasted as Hans pushes past, dumps his bags and asks for boiling water. ' Oh! ... Hello Dad. Where did you come from? Why no call to collect you at the airport? Come in. A cup of tea?'

'No thanks, boiling water will do. The water on the plane was lukewarm so I was stranded once my thermos ran out. I need some hot Rooibos. I know you don't have any but I've brought my own tea bags.'

'OK.' We sit. The kids hear talking and creep into the living room rubbing their eyes. Richard sees Hans, rushes up and hugs his legs. 'Hello Hans, where did you come from, the farm? Is the tree we planted when I came to visit big now? Is Franz looking after the dogs?' Hans smiles and ruffles Richard's hair. Lisa walks in sleepily and happy when Hans hoists her to his knees. Both turn to Brigitte and greet her in unison 'Hello Brigitte, did you come with Hans?'

After his cup of Rooibos, Hans leaves Brigitte with me and roams the house, 'Well do you have a bed?'

'Of course! Lisa can move in with Kate, we will move into her room. You can have ours.'

'Who is Kate?'

'She is our . . .'

'Oh don't tell me she is another of your waifs and strays. Why the hell do you always have to save others, what about your family? Your brother, perhaps, rather than having to save the world.'

'She is a foster child Dad. Fifteen and full of fun.'

'Well we won't be here long I want to go to Humpty Doo. I like the name, and then Katherine . . . I am researching Baobabs.'

'Oh!'

'Then maybe we can spend a weekend together. Where is Dave?'

'On his way to work. He leaves early to avoid peak hour when the trains are overcrowded.'

'So where should I put the bags? And where is the closest shop? I need some *'Aufshnidt'*. I will walk and buy as I am sure you have no money for cold meats and cheese.'

Brigitte talks for the first time. 'I will come with you Hans. I told you to let Jill know we were coming.'

Hans is back in our lives larger than life and on his terms alone. No consultation and without any planning. He is just here, and then he is not. Then back again with wonderful pictures of Boabs from the North to contrast with the Baobabs he is researching in South Africa. Dad always wanted to improve his knowledge and carefully studied anything that grabbed his interest. He read all about the mountains he climbed, knew much about art and particularly prehistoric rock art, and if an issue such as Peter's illness concerned him he would read everything he could lay his hands on about the subject. Now in 1982 he had been walking in the Northern Transvaal and encouraged by a friend decides to find out all he can about the world's Bottle tree species. I love this in my Dad and look forward to sitting with him and exchanging ideas about this, and about my learnings in my psychology course. I am even hopeful that we may have some exchange about Peter's condition and its effect on our family, but on the couple of occasions I try to talk about either his trees or my study Dad cuts me short. He is however ready to talk with Richard and Lisa.

On his return to Melbourne he brings with him a copy of Xavier Herbert's *'Poor fellow my country'* and for Richard, and for Lisa some Aboriginal children's stories wonderfully illustrated. For himself he has two stunning Aboriginal paintings rolled up and ready to take back to add to his ever increasing art collection in South Africa. 'Wow Dad, this is a beauty, very different colors from the ones I am used to. Looks like lots of nuts and fruit. I just love that vivid green and the olive grey background is beautiful. And this one is the more traditional riverbed but also wonderful colors. Where did you get these?' I ask.

Brigitte answers 'We got them just south of Darwin; they were painted at a mission alongside the Northern Highway.'

Hans asks nothing about our lives and while the children fall over themselves to engage him, grandpa is willing to educate, read and confront but not to listen. They sit at the dining room table where Hans has spread out his vast selection of photographs. They will do anything to help him with his research into the funny, fat trees that have more water than wood. 'Lisa do you see these fat trunks. They are filled with water. The tree pulls up moisture from the ground when it is wet and saves it for the months when it does not rain. That is how they stay alive.

Richard asks 'Are these ones that look like fat bottles from South Africa?'

'Yes, you can see the trunks are curved but this one I photographed while we were away in the North looks more like a coke bottle. Can you see they are taller and straighter?'

Hans also tells stories about the places he visited. The children love the stories and the way Hans plays with words. 'We drove for many miles and went to the towns whose names I liked. There was Humpty Doo and Borroloola, Milikapiti, Wurrumiyanga and Kakadu.' He takes out the map and together they trace his trip from one town to another. Hans gets both the kids to pronounce the names and the three of them giggle together as they enjoy the onomatopoeic sounds.

In the end Dad and Brigitte stay a week, expecting us to carry on as usual as Dad mulls, plans and writes his notes. He worries back and forth about his ability to research anything properly because he has 'no education', talks endlessly about the breathtaking rock paintings in Western Australia and the wonderful professor who is the world expert on Boabs. Dad is so anxious that he has not learned the rigors of scientific scrutiny that he examines and re-examines his findings. Finally, despite our vociferous protests that Dad should publish himself and get credit for his painstaking work, he decides that he will hand his research to the learned professor in the West on his return to Africa.

We go together to Wilson's Promontory and Hans strides off in front of us, vitally interested in everything he sees. He eats in the beauty of the place and insists on paying for everything.

He talks time and again about Peter. 'Remember that you have a brother who is in need of help.'

'Oh, has something happened?'

'No, he is still with Mandy the other '*meshuggeneh*' -

'Dad you shouldn't.'

- and they seem to get on well.' He continues as if I hadn't spoken. 'They live in a flat in Hillbrow along with three mangy cats. It smells of cat piss because the cat box is inside but otherwise it is pleasant. They look after each other but I need to visit to keep an eye on Peter and make sure he keeps taking his medication. The time will come when I am gone and it is your turn. I understand that you had to leave but this has made things very complicated.'

'Oh Dad!' and then to myself I mutter 'I was never able to make a difference. Every time I intervened, he tried to hurt me. Even if I was there, I would be powerless. Anyway, my responsibility lays with my children not my brother. Perhaps if you had listened to the doctors while there was a chance to get Peter to take responsibility for himself things might be better now.' These thoughts eat at me and I feel guilty but also resolute. My focus needs to be on my children.

We say goodbye at the house. He hates farewells and refuses to have us at the airport. In Perth, Hans hands over his extensive collection of photos and writings on Boabs and Baobabs, the professor publishes this comparative work and gets the kudos while Hans moves on to his next adventure.

I am left bewildered and out of breath. It was wonderful to see Hans, he enjoyed the kids but the same loneliness I'd always felt in my relationship with him remains. Despite now being almost thirty-five, his lack of interest in my life, or in speaking the few words needed to make a connection, still hurts. That night, I lie awake again, fearful but not sure why, wondering if I should write and tell him how glad I am that he came. I want my father to know I love him. I am desperate to hear him say the same to me but am scared to take the risk of being sentimental. Dad has never allowed such intimacy.

The South Africa I left behind

Like many other refugees I find it difficult to separate myself from the old country and often find myself thinking or dreaming of 'home.' So while I am working at Australian life I often hanker for South Africa. This is especially true when I hear from friends or comrades about my part in the history I have left behind.

One day I turn my mind to a time before we left, when I was campaigning with the Progressive Party and the advice office. I remember how living with unrest had became part of the government's psyche and that we had become accustomed to the *status quo* and almost took no notice of our growing paranoia. In the years leading up to our leaving white South Africa, whites did not talk openly about 'black danger' but they built higher walls, got a big dog and bought a gun to protect their family. While newspapers carried stories of growing unrest, it appeared as if the day-to-day lives of many whites did not change. Like ostriches they buried their heads in the sand.

But in fact Sharpeville (1960) and then Orlando (1976) were seminal milestones that galvanised hearts and minds of both the oppressed within South Africa and many in the outside world. Now in 1984 I read in the Australian papers that the South African government is continually reminded of 'black' people's strong antipathy to Afrikaans, the official language of government, through which every 'black' child is taught. Afrikaans has become a symbol of control and antipathy festers with children refusing to go to school and rioting until a state of emergency is invoked to suppress township revolts.

I hear about the international boycott of South Africa products, about the civil disobedience and demonstrations as thousands of 'black' people leave the homelands and flood the cities in search of work, about the world's increasing pressure on South Africa to end Apartheid and how some laws separating whites and non-whites in public places are being relaxed or repealed.

In 1989 I am in constant contact with friends in South Africa. Suddenly politics are electric. I remember a friend phoning in absolute exhilaration, 'Jill, remember that oaf, our State President FW de Klerk. He is talking to Mandela.'

In 1990 I got another jubilant call.

'The ANC has been unbanned and Mandela is free after 27 years. Can you believe it? Those bastards are changing.'

Having these events conveyed through friends or the media reminds me that I am cut off from the lifeblood of my history and the fruits of my political labour. I feel a great loss and long to be part of this extraordinary rebirth.

Now perhaps I can go back to South Africa and help rebuild. Do I dare suggest this to David and the kids who have toiled so hard to be part of Australia? I decide not.

By 1991 South Africa is constantly in the news. Then I sit in front of the TV, tears streaming down my face. I cannot believe it. The apartheid laws have been repealed and international sanctions against South Africa lifted. It is so hard to watch this alone. I feel totally alienated. My country has found a way to freedom without me. I will not survive. I have no place. This goes on for months. I am so depressed. I want to go home but I do not dare tell David. After all, I was the one to insist we leave.

I hide my sadness in cynicism. When the Nobel Peace Prize is awarded jointly to Mandela and de Klerk 'for their work for the peaceful termination of Apartheid and for laying the foundations for a new democratic South Africa' in 1993 I ignore the triumphant calls from home. When the TV is full of the first non-racial elections in 1994 I flip. Seeing blacks and whites queuing together to vote was real. Now I believed. Mandela, a black man, becomes the President and I am jubilant.

Later when I hear about the Truth and Reconciliation Commission on human rights crimes in the former government and the liberation movements during the apartheid era I am thrilled. My beloved homeland has come full circle and, like Germany, South Africa is working toward full and free democracy.

Now I long to return home to see the impact South Africa's new government has had on daily life. We have been in Australia for four and a half years, have Australian citizenship, David's work is going well and I have completed my psychology major and begun B.Ed. counselling. The children are settled in school, Richard in his final junior year and Lisa a year behind. We have furnished our house, had a couple of holidays and have some money to spare. I talk with Dave 'I have to go home and see what its like to live under a multiracial government.'

'You kept at me to leave and now you want to go back.'

'Everything I worked for has happened. I have to see it.'

' OK clearly you need to make the requisite visit home. I will stay and look after the kids for the first couple of weeks.'

'And then.'

'We can leave the kids with someone from church and I will join you for a week to visit the relatives.'

I am very excited about our trip. I hope so much to see South Africa flourish, all anger swept away by people like Mandela and Tutu, and that forgiveness in the form of the Truth and Reconciliation Commission has truly worked a miracle and set my country free. Scared that a bloodbath is inevitable.

***

I arrive at the airport and am welcomed by Des and Mike and fall into an easy conversation about family and friends. When we reach their home I sigh. I love this place with its cool grey slate floors, vibrant tribal rug and laid-back leather chairs. I enjoy the familiar paintings, endless cups of tea in Mike's well-established garden. This has always been my home away from home.

For three weeks I stay with Des in Pretoria seeing as many friends and compatriots as possible. I wonder that little has changed. Politics may be different but the conversations are not. Children are older and some have left home; each person I meet has aged but is otherwise unchanged. Friendships still run deep, the community is tightly knit and people are intricately involved in each other's live. Even those who do not believe are watched over by an omniscient God. Where the Australia I know is egalitarian and a social democracy, my South Africa has a religious soul.

I feel so comfortable and at home here. Was I right to leave. Part of me hopes to find my place in the new South Africa, to help strengthen this happy, integrated multi-cultural dream. I ask 'Are things going well in South Africa?' Many people don't answer but Julie is direct.

'Not yet, crime is high, AIDS is rife and people still cry against corruption.'

'Is it better then it was under Apartheid?'

'No but the leaders are now black.'

'And what about hope?'

'Perhaps for the next generation.'

With such comments I look beyond my yearning to come back and see that every door is always securely locked and on top of each three-metre wall there is now barbed wire or an electric fence reaching another half metre towards the sky.

A visit to the farm

Dave arrives and stays one night before he, Anneke my old school pal and I drive up to visit Hans, Brigitte and Peter on the farm. It is on the Transvaal escarpment three hundred kilometers from Pretoria. The farmhouse a picturesque soapstone cottage nestles on a small hillock surrounded by pine plantations. At its entrance stand two magnificent gums, sentinels reaching a full fifty metres into the sky-blue heavens. The plantations stretch to the horizon in the North and spill down to an oxbow in a stream that winds its way towards Ebenezer dam.

I have missed home and dream of being welcomed. I want to be in a place that I know and with those who care about what happens to Dave, the children and me. But alas, this doesn't happen. My family is the worst it has ever been.

Perhaps I have been away too long and my guard is down, perhaps I have forgotten Peter's manic attacks when he is agitated. He paces up and down as we sit on the verandah eating lunch. Each time someone speaks, he interrupts. It is exhausting. My old stress reaction returns and I get up and head for the toilet. I am dying to pee. Peter's arms flail as he rants unintelligibly as I pass.

After an outburst at Anneke I say, 'Hey Pete chill.'

Wrong. He picks up a bowl brimming with hot bolognaise and tips it over my head. 'Great!'

Dad says 'Leave Peter be' but the rage rises and I find it hard to restrain myself. 'Why is Peter always protected and me that has to keep my cool?' I look around for support and when none comes, I walk off into the pine plantation, dripping with sauce and march my anger into the ground. I walk in the cool deep shade of a maturing pine plantation, slow my pace and listen to the gentle ripple of the Broederstroom that drifts through grassy banks in wide sweeping oxbows. Finally I sit and sob myself dry, watch the stream, calm my breathing and finally turn around, and head for the farm perhaps three hours after rushing off into the forest.

As I arrive back just before sundown, clothes still stained with sauce, David and Peter are playing chess. Peter looks up, the black depth of his hollow eyes boring into my soul. This is the dark, hollow, haunting stare that disturbs my sleep.

Anneke is drawing quietly in the garden and Hans and Brigitte are having tea on the verandah. No sign of spilled bolognaise either in the kitchen or on the verandah. All is calm and I am determined that this will be the last time I react to Peter's uncontrolled behavior. I go into the bathroom shower, change, pack our things and return to the lounge, 'David I want to leave.'

Hans responds, 'Jill, you have it all, be more generous to Peter. Let it go. Peter can't help it.' Dave looks up and reaches for my arm. He does not want to be caught between us. I retreat deflated and go to bed. Thank God we live in Australia, and such visits are few and far between. After a night's sleep and a long chat with Dave I decide to try again.

We sit around the fire in the morning when Hans says, 'Where are the photos you stole?' I look at him blankly. 'Remember I sent you those snaps of you and Peter as kids. You never returned them.'

We were looking at our family histories in my counselling course and Dad had sent me an album of the first five or six years of my life. I was still working on this project, and had assumed I could hang on to the photos for a while but clearly, he expected them back on this trip. Again, Dad says, 'You've stolen my photos. They are mine!'

'Dad I'm sorry. I will post them as soon as I have finished my assignment.'

'You should have brought them.'

I am trapped. I have stolen nothing, merely borrowed photos, which Dad posted to me. Peter is becoming agitated so I say nothing more. Hans continues, 'So, am I to understand that you refuse to give them back?'

'No. I'll post them back on my return.'

Hans keeps on at me. 'You should have brought them with you.'

'Sorry Dad.'

'You never think about anyone but yourself!'

'Dad!'

'You . . .' I can't take anymore and rush from the room, climb into bed and pull the covers over my head. I sob into the pillow and do not respond to the knocks at my door. David comes in, sits on the bed and puts his hand on my shoulder but I just lie there. He talks to me gently, 'Are you OK? Say something. What do you want?'

'Nothing.' Dave sits beside me as I huddle below the covers, swallowing down my tears. After a while, he tries again 'Jill it's hard to sit by when you shut me out. Please talk to me. I love you and want to help.' I stare at him, unable to utter a sound. Eventually he walks out, and he and Anneke go off for a walk.

Peter creeps around outside the house and peers in through my window. Then he knocks, his haunted stare threatens, accuses, almost demands. A kaleidoscope of emotions flood through me, I remember times long before Peter's illness when we clung together scared of the total annihilation wrought by our parents. Is Peter reaching out to me now? Can I trust him? What should I do? Do I reach out to Peter or run for my life. I am too scared to do either. Dad will not accept my explanation about the photos. Unable to see any solution I again pull the blankets over my head and shut out this mad world.

The next day Hans expresses profound disappointment. He cannot understand why I make it so difficult for everyone else, especially Peter in his fragile state, 'I was merely asking you to remember that the photos are mine. Why must you always overreact?' The next couple of days are tense but pass without incident. It is a relief to leave. I know I left South Africa because of that visit from BOSS but here is definitely a reason to banish any thought of returning.

***

The next time Dave and I visit South Africa it is to see friends, David's family and for a holiday in the beautiful Cape Provence. However at my centre is a deep longing to reconnect with my homeland and see how it has changed since the Apartheid's demise. David and I plan a short, public visit with Dad and Peter to minimize any conflict.

We meet Hans, Brigitte, Peter and his partner Mandy at a steakhouse in Johannesburg. Five years after Mandela has become President, South Africa is well and truly free. I begin a conversation about the politics, thinking that this is a safe enough topic. Peter looks at me with blank vacant eyes, turns to Mandy and takes out his pill vial. For the next hour, they discuss their pills as we sit and watch, in awe. Uncharacteristically Dad says little and Brigitte chats politely about the vegetables and chestnuts she grows and harvests on the farm. Our meeting today is without incident or connection. In a way, I am grateful. Now at least there is no interaction between Peter and me and thus no fight. My brother is gone but the lunch is yummy and I love the onion rings I haven't tasted since my last visit to a South African steakhouse. Perhaps this uncomplicated, almost fatuous meeting is the base level from which we can begin again. I want with all my being to be part of a caring, feeling family; will this longing never stop?

The Hanns Katz Exhibition

Dad gives up on Boababs but never one to rest he turns his attention to reinstating Hanns Katz the artist he first met in Frankfurt in 1934. Katz paintings had hung in European art galleries alongside those of contemporary Existentialist artists such as Munch, Mark and Beckmann but as one of the 'Burnt' or 'Degenerate' artists his paintings disappeared during Hitler regime. In a catalogue dad compiled for the Hanns Katz memorial exhibition in 1992 he says:

'Hanns held lectures on art in his studio at home to which we were invited . . . For the first time in my life I heard of physics and higher mathematics. I learned about Einstein's theory of relativity and his concept of time, space and the fourth dimension. I was confronted with Hanns' philosophy of color and the question as to whether it could be the fifth dimension of space.'

Dad is bewitched and becomes deeply involved in Katz's ideas about communal living. At Katz's behest, he goes to Yugoslavia in 1935 to look for a possible place to settle. He reports back that the financial prospects of settling in Split are negative and his relationship with Katz cools.

When Dad is dismissed from a job because the company is *'Aryanised'* in 1936 he leaves for South Africa. Katz is another among the 537 penniless refugees who are on the passenger liner Stuttgart, which arrives in Cape Town later that year. Katz and his wife Ruth share a house with Dad and Mum. In reminiscing about Katz, Dad says,

'I do not for a moment doubt that Katz was the most educated, intelligent and talented person I have ever met . . . He was one of the great German Expressionists.'

After Katz's death in 1940, Dad helps Ruth, Katz's second wife, organize two exhibitions of his paintings one in 1941 and then a retrospective in the sixties.

South Africa is not ready for Katz. After the 1941 exhibition the paintings, mostly painted on board making them big and cumbersome, are stacked against a wall at the back of an art dealer's spare office. No care is given to the paintings and some are badly scratched and damaged. The paintings are still there in 1969 when David and I get married.

Dad contacts the dealer; Dave and I go together to the gallery, walk through the gallery into a cramped storeroom cluttered with paintings, sculptures and other *objects d'art*. We are directed to the furthest corner, handed a dusting cloth and begin the painstaking work of extracting about twenty paintings from the discarded collection. On hardboard, some are painted on both sides because when Katz was short of money he used any surface he could find. Once freed from their cramped quarters, we line pictures up along a gloomy passage and try to gain enough distance to examine each piece individually. I want them all but with little money David buys himself *'The Architect'* and as a wedding present for me, the right hand panel of Katz's most beloved work, a triptych painted in Germany in 1934/35. I truly love this painting and make it the centerpiece of any living space we inhabit.

Once again, in 1987, Dad is determined to claim Katz's place as an artist whose work should hang alongside other *'Moderns'* such as Marc, Beckman and Chagall. He moves heaven and earth towards this goal.

He sets himself the task of finding every piece of art created by Katz, writes to the owners and then travels to Los Angeles, New York, throughout Germany and to Israel. He speaks personally with many art collectors in South Africa.

He asks the owner of each artwork to loan their works to the Jewish Museum in Frankfurt for two years. Insurance policies signed, the artworks are shipped from around the world. A magnificent catalogue including beautiful plates of many works and Katz's history as teacher, artist and friend is compiled.

This huge logistical task comes together after years of painstaking work and the exhibition is opened on June 8, 1992. David and I are among the twelve select guests who meet to celebrate this auspicious occasion. Both my father's brothers are invited, the eldest from South America and the baby from Holland. For the first time in over fifty years, they come together to honor their heritage.

Dad is thrilled. He invites his twelve special guests to a dinner on the night preceding the opening, sits at the head of the table.

'Please celebrate the genius and pathos of Katz whose life epitomizes the birth of a new epoch bringing together philosophy, socialist idealism, humanitarianism, architecture, art, design and everyday life.' He read aloud from the catalogue introduction.

'You see in his expressionist painting Katz found a medium that brought his philosophy of life into reality. He was not content with the ordinary disposition of things in a workday world. He looked for universal law, for the eternal verities that he sought in philosophy and higher mathematics.

Hanns' pictures do not follow the normal laws of physics and space and he avoids the normal play of light and colour. By producing a conflict of colours Hanns presents a tragic tension that knows no compromise. He transfixes the essence of the tumult of his time in history with the forceful use of pastels or oils. The clash of dark blues, vermilions, greens, reds and charcoal against the stark ash grey light on faces and hands and the pastel shades that capture the translucence of glass conveys the agony and alienation, the cancer and madness of the world in which Hanns Katz has lived his life. The depth of horror and trauma portrayed in Hanns portraiture is at the same time obvious and transcending.'

This is the only time I remember Dad giving a speech and it is clear that commemorating Hanns Katz is significant. This is perhaps the apex of Dad's achievements. Without formal education, Dad finds validation through Katz's life, suffering, history and purpose.

Once the exhibition is opened and thoroughly enjoyed, Dad takes us on a tour of several other exhibitions. One captures the horrors of the Holocaust through word and graphic art, 'Look at these lead pencil drawings on tattered scraps of paper. These bodies laid out for mass burial will remind us forever not only of the horror of the death camps but also of how people used art to deal with their trauma.' From this exhibition, he takes us into a narrow alleyway through a medieval enclave and on to an exposition that demonstrates the hard, cold reality of the communist era in the Soviet Union. We leave these and follow speechless and stunned through parks and gardens along the Main River. Finally, Dad shepherds us into the modern city of Frankfurt. Here shiny, high, glass structures scrape the sky alongside burned out husks of bombed buildings. Germany has moved on into a thriving democracy that still finds space to include and respect the reminders of war and death.

***

One evening Hans and I walk together along the banks of the Main and I tell him how proud I am of his achievement and about the thrill of being included. He turns to me and for a moment, I see gentleness in his face. But then he turns away from me. He tells the river about Hanns, and of duty, and of Peter. He reminds me that there is no time for sentiment. 'We need to stay vigilant and remember responsibility.' We return to the hotel and the others. The moment I hoped for is past and my dream of intimacy is stillborn.

Prague

For just a few days Hans is jubilant, effusive and then he is suddenly overwhelmed by his achievement. Everyone has listened, followed and depended on him to lead the tour, choose the restaurants and plan excursions; to explore the beauty of Germany and the horror and the trauma of leaving it to Hitler's holocaust. They have applauded Hans' ability to survive and flourish, a proud custodian of the torch of expressionism. Now Dad wants to shun those who have listened and followed. Uncomfortable he wants to escape them and their heartfelt respect. Hans is not used to being a teacher.

On the fourth day of this gathering he worked so hard to create, he abandons further plans, forgets the company of the people he has brought together, and suggests an escape to Prague. Czechoslovakia is just beginning to open its borders to the west. Prague has been behind the Iron Curtain since the end of World War II in 1945 and Hans is intrigued.

Used to Hans' unpredictability, and curious and excited to explore magical medieval Prague, Dave and I agree, jump into our hire car and head South East. We reach Nuremburg in the late afternoon and seek out accommodation in a hotel opening onto the main market square. Settled, Hans leads us out to explore this neat walled town. He strides forth across the cobbled square, then suddenly stops and points. Here, in front of him is a tall, blond youth in Police uniform. The blood drains from Hans's face and it goes grey. He stares straight ahead and a shadow crosses his features. His mouth hangs open and hands shake. The youth looks dumbfounded and turns away but Dad does not move. I touch his elbow and he flinches still transfixed. 'Dad!' No answer. 'Dad?' He turns and speaks in German,

'I must leave this God forsaken place.'

'What is it Dad?'

'Nothing. Let's go up the hill towards the Kaiserburg. It was in this bourgeois hellhole that the Nazi rallies began in 1933. We cannot stay. We must leave immediately after breakfast tomorrow.' We continue sightseeing but Dad is intense, preoccupied and withdrawn, and for the first time he looks old.

He doesn't eat or sleep that night. Remembering Mum's reaction to a man wearing knee high, black boots like those worn by the Gestapo all those years ago in Munich I know what has happened to Dad and that night Dave and I talk again about the trauma of the Holocaust.

'Will Hitler's shadow never stop haunting my family?'

We arrive at the frontier mid-morning. Hans insists that we leave all discussion with guards to him. For an exhausting two hours, Dad shepherds us back and forwards from one queue to another, following the instructions of the officious uniformed guards. We are photographed, pay an exorbitant amount for four seven-day visas and eventually get the all-important stamp in our passports. Dad relaxes a little. Clearly, the suspicious questioning of officious bureaucrats has heightened Dad's anxiety. He had been named, shamed and expelled from his work because he was a Jew by officious Gestapo before he left Germany in the thirties.

We leave and immediately reduce speed as we now progress along a potholed single-width tar strip, the magnificent autobahns of Germany behind us. The farmlands either side of the road are overgrown and dilapidated.

Our first stop is in Pilsner where David wants a beer. Communism has ravaged what was obviously a thriving agricultural town. We wander through a muddle of tumble-down shops and I scrabble through the contents in an open tray of one dilapidated store and happen upon a lipstick called Lisa. Thrilled with the prospect of bringing home this small memento to my gorgeous, gentle, gregarious teenage daughter I squeak with delight and show it to David. Hans puts a heavy hand on my shoulder 'Respect the sadness of this place and its people.' Deflated and chastened, I put the lipstick back and slink out behind him. Humiliated, I watch myself and am wary about being over exuberant in any interaction. Dad and Mum have told us often to be aware and respectful of people who have struggled to survive or fled their homes because of uncaring regimes and dictators. 'You never know when it will be you who flees for your life!' How could I have been so unaware?

We arrive in Prague as the sun is setting over *Staromestske namesti*, the old town square, park and proceed on foot. As we

179

round a corner and see the square for the first time, I am transfixed. A fairy tale, the square is filled with twinkling lights and the sound of Mozart. With its beautiful Romanesque architecture, this square surrounded by ancient apartment buildings and magnificent churches must be one of the most beautiful historic sights in Europe. My father smiles, 'This is the Europe I have longed for!'

It is wonderful to have this opportunity. Hans leads us on a breathtaking journey of discovery. This man, my father, is a superb guide as he points out aspects of European tradition and politics only available to one who has been a part of its folklore and history.

He tells us about the architecture, art and artifice of many generations, plays with words and names, transfiguring the history he experienced or read about in newspapers. He points out each glaring clash between gracious buildings and the ravages of Communism. One still fixed in my mind is of a tenth century church scarred by a gaping hole closed off by an ugly rollup garage door.

We visit Prague castle and listen as a guide extols the virtues of Václav Havel the Czech playwright, essayist, poet, dissident and politician. We walk across the beautiful Charles Bridge as the sun is setting. Eat peanuts and sip wormwood vodka as we listen to haunting, guitar music and animated debate of young proprietors in a night cafe on a second floor balcony of a twelfth centuary building on the banks of the glistening Vltava. Their excited discussion of freedom and responsibility is an insight into a new generation whose parents have forgotten all but Communism. We change money in the backstreets of the city because official rates in the banks are outrageous and wonder at the starkness of the flat we live in while the tenants board with neighbors to earn a little extra cash.

For the first days, we eat food bought in Germany. When this runs out, we look for other supplies. Never before have I been confronted by so civilized an austerity. At the corner shop we hope to buy tea, bread and some cheese for dinner but find one dried out wedge on a shelf, no bread and only a minute pack of tea. There is no sugar. Again, I can see on Hans' face shadows of past remembrances.

On the fifth day, we wake to a cold morning, open the windows of the small apartment and look across a pall of smog. When we venture into the street, I cough. Hans is blue around the mouth, he can barely breathe. Sulfur dioxide from the brown coal water boilers and heating permeates the air so badly that we decide to leave and drive through East Germany and back to Frankfurt.

Outside Prague, we find a roadhouse where we eat the ubiquitous schnitzel, cabbage and potatoes before heading north. Within no time, we hit a stationary queue of trucks perhaps ten kilometres from the German border. Here we crawl, stop and crawl again for hours. We watch prostitutes ply their trade from truck to truck, drivers chat and Hans tells story upon story of the pathos of European history and of his love of this lost world. This intermingled with his devastating connection to the madness he saw in my mother and brother. While Dad talks about the madness he saw in them both, he adds that he had promised Else's father to look after Else and that he has planned for Peter's financial support in the future. He says that details are secured in the top drawer of his desk at the farm. 'Brigitte has the key. Another copy is lodged with the Standard bank in case something happens at the farm.' Having said this he returned to reminiscing.

'I remember once we went to a German youth rally. Here the Fuhrer ranted about his plans for Europe and the whole crowd including your *'meshuggeneh'* mother cheered. The look in her eyes was no different from your brother when he is high. Totally cut off from the world, consumed and crazy. I knew I would never have peace with her but she too was my responsibility.'

For the first time I am invited to share my heritage and with this I recognize that Hans is the quintessential European man fractured by the destructive power of a German Reich and a megalomaniac gone mad. We, his family, are the shattered shards he has left.

Selling my soul to save Hanns Katz

Having traveled to South Africa ahead of Dave I am met at the airport by the ever generous and accommodating Mike and Des. I am overjoyed to see them. Des and I hug and Mike gives me his same quiet smile. He looks at my trolley. 'My goodness Jill I hope I can fit that door into my car.'

I smile and say, 'I'm sooo sorry! Long story. It's for Hans.'

Twenty minutes later Mike finally fits my door-sized package into the car. Des and I sit each side of it in the back. He can steer but lucky it's an automatic, because there is no way, he could reach gear stick or handbrake. We head for Pretoria and Des, who cannot contain herself, asks, 'Jill what have you got there?'

I begin my long story. 'You remember that Katz painting Dave bought me as a wedding present?'

'Yes.'

'Well my father has bullied me for months to sell it to him. He wants it reunited with the other two panels of the triptych so he can sell the full set to the Guggenheim in New York.'

'That's a hard one!'

'Yup. Said I was being sentimental and stubborn when I refused'

'And'

'And as always he eventually won.'

'Oh.'

'Hans is desperate to reinstate Katz as a great painter, so I had no choice really. I just had to bring it with me.'

'Always something with your family isn't there?'

'He promised me another painting. I don't like it half as much, but it's also a Katz. David is very hurt that Dad talked me out of my wedding gift. I feel so guilty.'

'Not again Jill?'

'But a little excited! It will hang in one of the world's most famous galleries. Also the $20,000.00 he is paying will help with the mortgage.'

This double bind is just another one of Hans's family specials.

Hans comes within a day. He doesn't chat. Consumed with his task he says a perfunctory, 'Hello. No time for tea. I'll see you at the farm week after next Jill. Pleased the painting got here in one piece' and whips it off for shipment to New York where it has been ever since. I am now fond of the replacement and pleased that Katz is again noted as one of the Burnt Artists whose contribution remains long after Hitler's demise.

TUG OF WAR

When we first arrive in Australia I set aside personal concerns as the family toils together to build a new life, finding and furnishing a home, building some connection to community and learning about our new country's expectations of new Australians. Once we have some stake and feel secure in relation to David's work I allow myself the luxury of wrestling with my past. I now realise that leaving South Africa and my history behind me will take more then merely adjusting to the new.

For many years I feel torn. South Africa with its constant in your face racism fits so well as a backdrop to my schizophrenic, traumatised family of origin. Its pull after the fall of Apartheid is almost greater as it is in this cauldron that the working through of hatred and fear is truly tested.

Then everything changes. Mandela is released from prison after twenty-seven years.

Transfixed by television footage of President Botha shaking hands with Mandela. Listening to Mandela's colossal humility, strength and determination to build a new transcendent South Africa has me aching to return and be part of this national rebirth but I cannot because I have dragged my family here and they are now settled.

I determine to stay; the struggle to assimilate, accept my family of origin and let go of my anger is exhausting.

Growing up Australian Style

'Richard, put on your school shoes.' I say to my ten-year old son.

'They hurt.'

'Come here. Let's have a look . . . They're fine, plenty of room for your toes and no blisters so what's the problem. I wore leather school shoes and so did you in South Africa.'

'But Mum!'

That afternoon I see Rich pulling his black shoes out from under a bush and replacing his sneakers. Oh well one less thing to buy and to hell with smelly feet. 'I'm starving Mum, where's the bread?'

'Not too much Rich, it'll be dinner soon. Any homework?' I turn to Lisa 'How was school? Not too much chatting in the back of the class? Know where Kate put her jeans? They need a wash.'

After dinner Kate huffs off to her room to listen to her music, Dave dozes in front of the fire, and Lisa, Rich and I sit down to our homework at the kitchen table. When not studying, I write to Des knowing that she will let everyone know how well things are going.

'Hi Des,

Miss you. Hope everyone is well.

We've stopped church hunting. We'll not find any who wish to build their lives together as we did.

We now meet with other families every Wednesday evening to eat, talk and pray but it's not the same. I long to be understood. We are so different. I wish they would take us on trust. Perhaps, with time.

Life here leaves little time for contemplation. I'm always running between judo for Rich, netball for Lisa, shopping, washing and cleaning, but it's great that my classes are either during school hours or when Dave is home from work so I can always be there when the kids get home from school.

A couple of school mums have come over. They think I'm from outer space with pictures on the walls and stacks of books and no furniture. Lucky Aussies like aliens.

We have finally furnished our family room and I am thrilled. The thick hand woven rug we bought together looks wonderful below our new lounge setting. The low-slung simple wooden frames holding dark brown leather cushions. The fireplace they face is of twice-fired sandstock brick. The muted ash panelling across the room is the perfect backdrop for the Katz flower panel and the loose weave curtains frame our small patchy lawn, which struggles to survive under three pencil thin twenty metre gums. The only problem is that the room has five entrances all of which need to be furniture free which makes it impossible to move the furniture into any other position. Well as you are not here I probably won't experiment anyway. Dave will be pleased; less lugging furniture from one place to another, and less giggling.

Dad wrote the other day and it's great that Peter and Mandy seem well settled in their flat and support each other. They have three cats and treat them like kids but that is cool. It's fantastic that I don't need to worry about Peter and can get on with building my own life. When we talked for his birthday he was a friendly robot. Life consists of Mandy, cats, cricket and telly. He asks about us but doesn't listen to my reply.

Maybe I should have left South Africa sooner. I feel like an almost whole human being here and am much too concerned with study, Life Line where I get counselling experience, spending weekends exploring Australia or meeting people from David's work or my study to feel scared. Almost no dreams now. What a relief.

Oh well back to study before the kids catch me sneaking away from it.

Love to all, Jill'

***

Lisa bounces into the room and says 'Look Mum what do you think.'

'What the hell are you doing Lisa? What's in your ear?'

'Oh! Kate put it into my ear so that I could look realistic. Do I look like Boy George?'

'Is that a safety pin?'

'Oh come on Mum chill. Kate sterilized the needle in a flame before she pierced it."

'Great. Kate come here, now!'

Life bumps along and Dave and I often marvel at how Aussie we are. We are now citizens. The kids are well adjusted and happy, and Australian politics make perfect sense. Thanks to Whitlam I am a psychologist in training and get a job that fits perfectly with parenting.

In my first position, I become a solid reliable counsellor but not content with listening well, I decide to work on myself. I have always felt a little mad; I had to be to survive the lunacy of my family. At school, I spoke with Anneke who joined in prank after prank as we sought support by acting out. When Mum was called in to see my head mistress because Peter tore up my homework, I was disciplined but not heard. At university in South Africa, I was too scared to study psychology. Anyway, now as a counsellor myself I need to get a feel for what it is like to have counselling and decide to visit a psychiatrist. The first guy lasts all of four months, which is pretty bad seeing that he is Freudian and expects clients to come at least weekly for ten years but I cannot accept his absolute silence. On the fateful day that I stop seeing him, I arrive ten minutes early so have the car cleaned. This takes twenty minutes and I arrive fifteen minutes late. I'm incensed when he dares interpret my lateness as avoidance. Anyone can see that I am merely making good use of my time.

My second foray into therapy is with a psychiatrist who looks the spitting image of the Katz portrait to whom I told my earliest secrets. This work is part of my training as a psychologist and I take it very seriously. For one and a half years, I go three times a week. Two years is seen as the minimum for a student to get a comprehensive understanding of what it is like to be a client.

I remember very little about this therapy. No feelings, excitement, nor insight into my behaviour, but I was impatient on many occasions at allegations I was not taking analysis seriously if three or four minutes late. Looking back I smile, I am a stickler for time and am usually early.

My only clear memory is that when I find my analyst is not Jewish I lose interest. In the session I sit upright on the couch, turn, look the analyst directly in the eyes and say 'I do not have time to waste while nothing happens. Thank you, I will not be back.'

'But in analysis we take time to talk about finishing. Ours is an important relationship.'

'Well I don't have the time or the inclination. We are painting our house and have a deadline.'

'Ah! You are resistant and resentful. You need . . .'

'No I just don't have endless time and money to spend on a process that gives very little and costs a lot. Now please can I pay what I owe?'

'Well I will give you time to get back to me before I fill your place.'

'Not necessary! Thanks.'

I pay the exorbitant fee and despite continued protestations I walk out never to return. I guess I do learn that I have better things to spend my money on.

What might the next six months have revealed had I stayed?

Working through work

To my very great surprise I look back over my twenty-five year career in Australia and become aware that I have systematically if unconsciously used work to peel away one after another layer of childhood trauma.

Have I taken this long to unmask the Boogieman?

***

My first step is to learn about family relationships and then of course to practice, practice, practice.

I sit in a session with a husband and wife. The man says to me 'We always fight about how to stack the dishwasher, she just has no idea!'

I respond 'OK! Let's start at the beginning. Please tell me about your Dad Simon?'

'What the hell has that got to do with our problems?'

'I'm not sure yet but we won't know until we begin.'

'Start with her then.'

Once settled and confident as a counsellor, I begin focusing on relationships where domestic violence is the issue and, surprise, I continually worry about its impact on the children.

I have a doll's house in my counselling room and children often play there as Mum or Dad or the couple speak. Sometimes it is obvious from this play that things are bad. When this happens I ask for time alone with the children. 'Hey Josh. What are you doing?'

'Daddy is hitting Mummy.'

'And where are you, Josh?'

'I'm under the bed with Jenny, hiding, but yesterday Daddy saw me and hit me too and when I told him not to hit Mummy he cried and ran away.'

Taking the children's concerns and fears back to parents often motivates the couple to look at their relationship honestly and begin the painstaking and difficult work of stopping the violence.

Openly recognising the violence and talking to the children about this is central. If only someone had helped my floundering parents.   My focus on the children comes from intimate knowledge of their helplessness and lack of a voice, and my ability to sit with conflict from direct experience with my own family of origin.

For many, working with violence is treacherous but I feel grounded in this work and as I watch and help control what is revealed within my counselling room I sleep more soundly at night.

Hans dies

It is 1995. Both Richard and Lisa have left home but come home most Sundays for dinner. I love these evenings where Richard holds forth endlessly about philosophy and power politics and Lisa, not bothered to fight her brother for airtime, chats quietly to me about Socialism and the politics of those less fortunate, community development or her latest foray into managing all the backstage elements of student theatre productions. Their lives have everything to offer and they want us to enjoy their achievements.

With the kids gone, I fully embrace my career and am studying again. My time is full but David is not happy. His work is in the doldrums and he moves through life in hunched, brooding silence. He roams about the house without purpose and says I am consumed with work and study and have no time for him.

**

I sit on the top step, phone in hand and talk to Dave who is at the bottom. 'That was Brigitte, Hans is in hospital. It sounds bad. I think he will die. I need to go home and see him before this happens.'

'Why? You found him so difficult.'

'Because he is my dad! I have now learned so much about repairing family relationships and want to say I understand his pain and respect his constant striving to help Peter live as well as he can. To tell him I love him despite our struggles. To say goodbye.'

'Go if you must. Perhaps Lisa can go with you.'

I rush to get everything ready. Lisa wants to come. With no support, it takes three days to get ready. It could have been two if Dave had helped.

The plane is delayed in Zimbabwe, we arrive seven hours after schedule, and Des and Mike are there. They have waited all this time. We go to their place for breakfast and I am about to phone and hire a car but Mike says, 'Take mine.'

We jump in and head for the farm three and a half hours drive away.

As we drive north, we talk about Hans. Lisa has not seen him for years and remembers only the man who played with words, talked about trees and strode off in front of us towards the top of a mountain with us panting behind. She says 'You always seemed scared of him Mum.'

'I let him down by leaving South Africa when I was supposed to look after Peter and I never got on with Brigitte. She stole Mum's place and told me things about Dad and their marriage that I didn't want to know. He was quite cruel to her. But Dad! I love him and I hate him. The way he judges me. I never feel good enough, I must tell him I love him before he dies. I am a fraud not a psychologist if I don't. How can I help others when I can't get my own relationships right.'

Lisa strokes my arm. 'Hope he'll listen Mum. You never said much about your parents but I know they hurt you. Is that why Peter is mad?'

'Oh Lisa! I don't know.'

***

There is plenty of parking under spreading jacarandas in Dorp street. We jump out in front of Pietersburg Hospital and walk quickly towards the sprawling single storied brick structure with high, bared windows and surrounded by an imposing concrete wall topped with a tunnel of barbed wire. Lisa walks ahead of me goes to the help desk where a receptionist, in crisp white uniform asks us who we wish to see. She looks at her computer and then back at us 'Are you relatives?'

'Yes I am his daughter.'

'Sorry your father died an hour ago. His body has been transferred across the road to the undertaker.'

I am devastated.

Across the road, a sad looking funeral director asks if we wish to view the body. I avoided seeing Mum's body so only remember her face ravaged and in agony as she fought having a tube forced down her throat. This time I must look. 'Yes.' He ushers us into a room where a funeral dirge plays quietly from tinny speakers. The lights are dim and there is a slight sulfurous smell of embalming fluid. Hans's body lies in an open pine box.

Dad's face looks composed and peaceful, eyes shut and no expression in the smoothed out wrinkle lines. I touch his cheek. It feels like a piece of meat. He has gone. He is definitely dead and all the rehearsed lines are of no avail. This body will hear nothing. Lisa and I stand together disconsolate.

Dad will be buried and Lisa and I want to attend this ceremony so continue the fifty kilometres to the farm, exhausted and with a funeral to prepare. I phone Dave to tell but cannot reach him.

We wind our way up the worn dirt track now blocked from the sun by a canopy of a mature pine plantation. As the car churns across the final gravelly incline beneath four huge Mountain Ash and onto the grass in front of the old soapstone cottage, Brigitte walks out onto the balcony to greet us. Her face is grey and drawn. 'Now finally you arrive when your father is dead. Well come in, I have prepared a room for you.'

We enter; Lisa and I are almost too tired to speak.

Brigitte gives us a few minutes to gather ourselves after our two-day journey and then explains 'Your father was on a ladder at the back of the house cleaning out the gutters when he slipped and fell. He hit his head against the rock outside the back door and collapsed. He rose, came inside but then tripped again that night and hit his head on the bookshelf. Uncle Piet helped me get him to hospital but it was too late.'

Lisa says 'It must have been difficult for you.'

Brigitte turns and faces me not Lisa 'I don't need sympathy or fuss. Your father was a morose old man and our marriage had long gone sour. All that interested him was sex, blazing trails through old growth forests and his art. He seldom spoke to me except about Peter and spent most of his time in his study with the door closed or out slashing through forest with Secondo. I want him cremated and only a small wake at the house. No commemoration or long farewells!'

'Brigitte, Lisa and I have are exhausted; let's discuss funeral arrangements tomorrow.'

She shrugs 'Sure but I won't change my mind. Very few people liked your father. They hated his politics, saw him as a 'brother of the blacks', and got sick of his ignoring them so let's just get it done.' She turns to Lisa and smiles 'I lit the fire this morning, your shower will be hot. Rest well.'

Exhausted we shower, fall into bed and sleep soundly till morning.

Next morning I phone Peter. Mandy answers, I ask her if Peter is well. 'Yes.'

I ask to speak to him and begin 'Dad's fallen off a ladder.'

'So . . . he is dead, isn't he?'

'Yes Peter . . . are you OK?' He is mute.

'Peter?' Still no response so I ask for Mandy. Nothing. 'I'll call when I know about the funeral. If you need to speak before, call.'

At breakfast I suggest the small community hall as a memorial venue but Brigitte is adamant 'No fuss. No one will come anyway.'

'Well?'

'We can have Hans cremated and spread his ashes in the forest. I will have an afternoon tea here on the farm and let people know through our phone tree. I want this done quickly.'

I let Peter know. 'OK Jill, maybe I'll see you in Jo'burg. I won't come to the farm. Goodbye.'

Brigitte makes arrangements and four days after Dad's death we arrange furniture in the main room, gather armfuls of flowers and tidy the verandah, so people can sit there or spill onto the lawn. Brigitte bakes scones and German shortbread. With everything ready, we sit out in the sun and await the first mourner. My stomach churns. How could I love and respect Dad, and yet be so angry and hurt, and what on earth will I do about Peter? Had I ever agreed to be responsible for him and if so what did this mean with me in Australia and Peter here? My family therapy had certainly not prepared me for dealing with this. As we wait endless minutes, I became more and more agitated. Not even Peter is here. I wish he were.

Is Brigitte right? Has Dad no friends.

194

Finally, a few people come and stand around awkwardly talking about 'mountain business.' I have let Brigitte take the running so far but this is no funeral so now I take over. I welcome people and speak a couple of tentative sentences to the very small gathering. I talk about my parents leaving Germany, finding South Africa beautiful but hating the politics. I talk about Dad's first assents, about his love of art. I say also that he and Brigitte married, and made the farm their home after Mum's death. I end with, 'Goodbye Dad, Sorry I wasn't here to say goodbye in person. Now would anyone like to speak?'

There is a long silence and then a woman says. 'Hans always said good things about my paintings. Said I should exhibit.' But then others talk and I am horrified. A neighbor stands. 'He was a cranky old bastard. Always complaining. Now perhaps no one will fuss about the bridge.' Another answers 'Pain in the ass telling us how to manage the blacks. Don't know how you put up with him Brigitte'

Why had these people bothered to come. I wish I hadn't unleashed this vitriol. The comments temper but keep coming with only one more positive. 'Hans had enormous energy. He and Secondo laid out all the walking tracks in this region. He will be remembered for that.' Finally, Brigitte says, 'Enough! A cup of tea anyone?'

I am shocked by what has happened. Why did these people come and why did I expect a normal farewell. My Dad tied me in knots so why not others? But still I expected people to consider our feelings.

The only comfort in these few days comes from Lisa, my beautiful, strong, gentle, compassionate girl. I don't know why I am so grief-stricken. How do I make sense of this man who fought so hard to resist fascism and protect the weak but humiliated and hurt me? 'Lisa I'm lost. Can't get Dad and he is the only person who knows how I feel about Hans.'

Well, tell me Mum. It's too late to protect me now. I've heard what the mourners said and I've always wondered why we didn't see much of Hans. Were you protecting us?'

'Guess so. He always made me feel guilty. I was never good enough. Even when Peter was a total write off, he said I didn't care. He never understood that Peter hurt me physically. I was supposed to just be strong and manage him and myself. Why are the men in my life never there when I need them? Why does it always fall to us women to deal with the hard stuff? I am so scared of Peter, how can I be responsible for him? I never promised Dad but I know he expected it, I want to speak to Dave where is he?'

'Mum. I'm here and you'll be home soon. Dad is different from Hans, he cares about us and I love you. You're a great Mum.'

I keep trying to contact Dave but he does not answer and I get scared. Should I have stayed? Dave said this was not a good time for him. What did he mean?

***

Brigitte says she is fine and we return to Pretoria, phone Peter and arrange to meet him. Lisa and I drive to Hillbrow and are just about to go up to Peter's flat when he strides up clothes unkempt, hair knotted and awry, face contorted, blood congealed on his cheek and his eyes wild. He looks wired. 'Let's go.'

'Go where Peter? Are you OK?'

'Fine. I had a fight with Mandy so let's just get out of here.'

'Oh! You invited us to see the flat.'

'Well Mandy won't let me in, even with you in tow.'

'Peter you look like hell. How is Mandy? Can I at least see if she is OK?'

'She's fine. She called her daughter who's coming. Let's just get out of here.'

'I would like to go up. What's your flat number?'

'176 but she won't answer the door to you either.'

We go into the white-tiled lobby of a twenty-story residential apartment block and press the up button. Peter paces as we wait and bangs against the mirrored interior wall of the lift while it travels ever so slowly to the seventeenth floor. The flat's front door has been kicked in. I turn to Peter 'Your handiwork?'

'I won't be locked out of my own flat!'

I knock and Mandy answers. She looks fine. 'Oh hello Jill, I'm not letting that maniac in until he's calmed down.'

'Fine. We'll be out for the afternoon.' I take her into the lounge 'Will you be safe after that?'

'Yes I can call the police or my daughter. Just need space.'

We go back to the car. 'If I'd hit her she'd know about it!' Arms flailing he demonstrates his right hook and hits his fist hard into his palm and gets into the front seat. Lisa looks at me and gets in the back, 'Are you OK Mum?'

'Yup, just need a loo.'

I head for the nearest public place I can think of with a toilet and jump out. 'I'll be back in a jiff.'

I don't want to leave Peter with Lisa in the car park, even with a couple of other people close by. I return quickly and head for a café in a shopping centre close by. We grab a quick coffee and go on to the trustee who will be managing Peter's affairs. Lisa sits outside his office and waits. It's hard to concentrate with Peter weaving back and forth. The executor of Dad's estate tries to offer condolences but Peter wants to hear nothing about Hans, his death or how this affects his future.

I have a go. 'Peter, Dad wanted this meeting to put your mind at rest.'

'Help? I'm on my own now. Just me, my voices and maybe Mandy.'

'Will you miss Dad?'

'I didn't like him telling me what to do. Who will look after me now?'

'That's why we are here Peter. Dad made sure there was money to look after you.'

'Don't want to talk about it.'

The executor speaks. 'Peter you can come and see me about money anytime, and I will look after it for you. I will arrange an allowance and help you with bills.'

'Let's go Jill.' Peter keeps pacing but I try once more.

'Peter did you hear Mr. C.'

'I want to leave.'

'OK. Thanks Mr. C.'

Mr. C says 'I will be in touch." but Peter has already left the office. Lisa watches him trying to open the car door without keys. I rush out. 'Thanks Mr. C, must go.

On the way back I try yet again. 'I'm sad about Dad, are you?'

Peter ignores me 'Are you going to the Magaliesburg? I will visit you in Australia.'

'Drop you home or should we take you to Tara?' I'm still worried about his earlier fight but Peter seems calmer and Mandy has a plan if things get out of hand. 'Home's fine. Mandy and I will watch the cricket.'

We go up to the flat but Mandy is out, a note saying she'll be back later. Peter closes the door without a goodbye and we return to Des and Mike's home.

The minute we are back in the car Lisa begins. When he climbed into the front of the car, I was worried Peter would hit you. His arms were flying all over the car. Looked like he was on speed. Why'd you leave us alone when you went to the loo?

'Sorry! I'm all over the place. I don't understand myself. I'm sad and I know I will miss Dad but I couldn't get cope with him and now Peter. I don't know what to do. Part wants to look after him and the other knows I don't understand the first thing about him. I'm so sad.'

'Love you Mum, I'm sad too and Peter is as mad as you said he was.'

Des wraps us in the warmth of her family and our friends, and within a ten days of setting out to bury Dad I am back in Melbourne. Lisa stays on a while. On my return, David is at the airport. I run to him expecting him to open his arms to me. 'Hi Dave. My dad is dead.' He turns away 'I know. It's late, let's get back to the house.'

Trying to get a grip

On the way home David is distant but I'm too tired to worry.

Over the next week I go back to work and study, and tell myself that everything is fine. The only change is that Dave now plays squash after work, happily does shopping on Saturdays and is often home late. He accompanies me on one occasion to sort out Dad's will, but is otherwise detached.

Dave what's going on? You won't talk. What's wrong?'

'Nothing. You father may have died but you have work and study, have no interest me and don't care about my work so I don't talk. There's no point. You don't listen to me'

'So speak and I'll listen.'

'Not now I'm off to squash and I don't want to be late.'

I swallow. Dad said soon after David asked him for my hand in marriage. 'You'll never hold any man!' These words had hurt. Now they seem true I've lost him and David won't even try talking.

Weeks pass, I try my learned listening techniques but Dave does not change so I talk to my friend Ilana who suggests I confront Dave but I have tried. I have also tried to share my stomach-turning mess of emotions at losing Hans. Of dreams filled with him extolling Katz, climbing, protecting Peter, sharing his political passions and the haunting nightmares about Dad asking for the impossible and finding me wanting. Not once does Dave listen.

Months pass and I fill the gaping hole with work. Then it dawns on me that maybe our marriage is like those I work with where the one partner is blind to what is happening for the other and I ask 'Are you having an affair.' His answer is a flat exhausted 'No.' Finally, after I say I can't go on like this, he tells me he has developed a friendship, not an affair.

'Stop lying, you're driving me mad!'

'OK I am.'

'Who, where did you meet, was this while I was burying Dad?' My voice rises with each question.

'Met her before you left but we spent time together while you were away.'

'In my house?'

'Yes.'

'And you fucked her in my bed?'

'Yes.'

'Oh I can just see it. How often?' I have heard that illicit sex is best in the marital bed. 'Go to her. Get out of my house now.'

'But I love you.'

'Sure. Just get out.'

'No Jill this is my house too and I love you, we've just lost the plot. We can work it out.'

'Well phone her now. Finish it.'

He does.

The next thing I know she is at my door. When I answer her insistent knock she pushes past me, runs to Dave, throws her arms around him and looks up into his eyes pleading. 'David we talked about this, we love each other. She doesn't care about you!' He looks blankly past her arms limp at his side as she to begs him to go with her.

As I watch this woman clinging to Dave I see David with his mother. She is begging his forgiveness and love after disappointing him yet again. At that moment his lover is the spitting image of David's mother. My mouth drops and David recognizes what he has not seen until this moment. He stands frozen and then gasps 'Oh no!' She clings to him and begs.

For me time has stood still but now I know what to do. I grab this imposter by her arms, manhandle her to the door and throw her out. In this scuffle, her glasses fall off and break.

When I return David said, 'Oh God, you saw it didn't you. I've been fucking my mother.'

***

Now begins week after week of recriminations. I have been deserted in my time of most need. David says I abandoned him long ago to my work and study.

Day after day I lock myself away in my office unable to focus on any work. I had believed that Dave and I would do marriage better then my parents because we loved each other but now love is simply not enough. My Dad was right 'Marriage is a contract. No more. I married your Mum because I promised her father to look after her. Remembering this made our marriage bearable.'

I have failed. My love could not hold my man, Dad was right and I am bereft.

Dave says over and again that I never listen and do not respect him. He spends less and less time with me, and when together he is morose, sarcastic, blaming, depressed and distant.

Eventually I say 'David it was almost better when you were having the affair. At least then there was a reason. What do you want from me? Please talk. You know I'm trying.'

He slinks off to bed. Next morning I say 'I'm drowning. I listen but you won't speak. I feel as trapped as I did when I was at home with Peter. I will pack this weekend.'

Dave says nothing.

That afternoon I get a call at the office. Dave says 'Please come home' and something in his voice is so desperate that I drop the phone and rush to my car. When I get home fifteen minutes later David is in a foetal position on the floor. He can't speak. I sit down next to him and cradle his head on my lap. We are together like this for a long time. Finally David cries. Later he sits up and says 'Please don't leave, I need you.'

'But'

'Jill I know you are trying but you don't hear what is going on inside. I'm empty, work is disintegrating, I don't know who I am.'

'Sounds awful, Dave but if you want me to stay you must get help. Let's go together.'

'I can't go on. Please don't leave.'

I know from my many years of couples work that men often make promises to get help when they are desperate but change their minds once the wife agrees to stay. But I decide to stay at least until Dave is on an even keel. I would not forgive myself if something happened and I had not tried.

'I will stay if we get help.'

Finally he looks at me and I see fear in his eyes. 'Dave I love you.' He sees my tears and says, 'OK, perhaps I should go on my own first.'

After two visits to the psychiatrist I am asked to attend a joint session and here David tells me that he has been clinically depressed for years. After establishing that David will continue treatment, the psychiatrist suggests I see a colleague to deal with my own grief and past trauma. We discuss the therapy model this worker uses and I am skeptical but the psychiatrist confronts me 'Why did you agree to come if you won't take my advice. That's pretty self defeating.'

'Well . . .'

'This treatment is new but I have seen some good results.'

'OK I'll go.' When we leave, I book an appointment.

Dave now has counselling weekly and several months later, when my treatment is done, Dave and I have one further session together. We talk about our relationship both hopeful about our future together. The psychiatrist wishes me well 'Jill when you are angry with Dave give him a Chinese bangle. It hurts like anything but does little harm and your anger, as you know is normal.'

EMDR - Treatment for Trauma

I attend ten wonderful but very difficult sessions where I have intensive support as I looked at nightmares of the Boogieman that are back full blown and terrifying. In these sessions, a gentle lady teaches me something totally new about counselling. 'Jill I want you to visualize your own special cloak of invincibility. Can you see it?'

'Sort of.'

What color is it?'

'Purple.'

'And the texture?'

'Silk. Very fine but very tough.'

'Is it warm?'

'Not really, but beautiful and I love its feel.'

'OK as long as it's strong. Whenever you feel scared, wrap it around yourself as protection, and I will help you control your breathing and calm yourself. Are you ready?'

'Not sure.'

'OK let me tell you a more about what we will do. I will move my finger in front of you like this.'

Louise shows me how she will move three fingers slowly from left to right and back for the time she wishes me to visualize. 'Sounds ridiculous.'

'Perhaps but try it anyway. As you follow my fingers, tell me what you see. It's like a movie running in front of your eyes. I will watch carefully and if I see distress, I will help you put on your shawl and calm you down. I am right here with you and won't let you become overwhelmed.'

'But when I remember some things I can't breathe, like I'm being swallowed alive by terrible memories. Like I'm suffocating.'

'That's why I'm here and I won't take you places you can't go.'

Slowly I agree and then watch as Louise, a wonderful lady, waves me through my most difficult experiences like Peter's fire,

Else's drunken ravings and that unbearable visit to the lock up ward and finally David's betrayal. When things get too painful, I wrap myself in my pretend cloak, and try to breathe as I listen to the soothing voice of my own special guardian who is present when it hurts most. After such sessions, I struggle to drag myself back to reality. I have not been hypnotized but am in a very different reality. On one occasion, I drive into a pole as I leave. Luckily, not at breakneck speed and no one is in the way.

Some movies are too terrifying to run, but there are also some lost memories that are quite fun, like squirting a burglar in the eye with a water pistol thinking he was a cat fighting outside my window. His screams of horror at being violated were funny. I remember yelling after him, 'Come again any time!'

***

Slowly Dave and I get it together. We tell both children and they spend time with us as we rebuild our family. My work takes less priority as we buy a beach house and spend time together turning this house into a new home. We call it '*Miklat*' the Jewish word refuge. David chose it to capture his new intentions.

I have had no therapy since and am coping OK, except that the nagging longing for recognition persists; and sometimes the madness lurks, as if I can choose this path if normal gets too hard.

No therapy has helped explore my issue of responsibility for Peter but then I have not been ready to think about this until now.

Peter, Peter, Peter

Any relationship with Peter since Dad's death has been bizarre. Dad's imperative to take responsibility jangles in my head and my inability to fulfill this obligation haunts me. How can I look after Peter while living in Australia, I won't live in South Africa and I know Peter can't come here.

The ultimate truth is that Peter's life will be no different wherever he lives.

***

Peter's calls are sometimes good and sometimes not. Good means he says almost nothing but he is alive.

'Hello Jill'

'Hi, how are?

'Fine . . .'

'OK. What are you up to?' Nothing. Has Peter put the receiver down and wandered off. Is there a reason for this call, some connection perhaps?

'Is anything happening?' Silence. 'Lisa is . . . '

'Not really interested . . . '

'So?'

Silence and eventually, 'OK then Jill . . . ' another silence. Finally, I hang up. Perhaps he just wanted to hear my voice? Who knows?

Less good are, 'Hi Jill. I'm fine what's up?'

'Hi, All's well here. Been quite busy with work and I have started writing. Dave . . . '

Peter responds 'I am going to write a book. It will be published by Penguin and be translated into . . . '

'Anything new?' I try to steer away from this fantasy.

'Get my passport organized now. Mandy wants to go via Hong Kong and book a ticket via Emden so I can see the Katz pictures. Dad said . . . ' and he's off again. His psychiatrist has told Peter he cannot travel.

I reluctantly listen, then hand the phone to David if he's around. He doesn't feel guilty and is better at chatter. These calls reminded us of Peter's plight.

When Peter doesn't call for months I worry, knowing he is so depressed he cannot reach out or has been so high that someone has had him committed.

The difficult conversations include a 3AM call ten years after Dad's death. A shrill ring wakes me. I shake myself from sleep. It is a hysterical Mandy. Peter has hit her. Peter is in the room with a pan and is still ranting. I talk quietly in the hope that Mandy will calm 'Call the police. I can do nothing from here.'

Peter grabs the phone yelling. I wait for him to stop 'Peter this is bad for you both. Get out before you really hurt her.'

'Why should I go, it's her fault she . . .' he screams incoherently for several minutes and I say nothing. When he gets no response, he finally shouts, 'Fine, I will get out, but this is my place.'

'Go and tell the police what has happened.'

'You don't understand she . . .'

'Peter this is no time to explain. Go!'

The door slams and Mandy is back on the phone. 'Mandy, call the police now while he is out.'

'But I love him.'

'Love him?'

'We both love animals, the garden, watch TV together, check our medication. We're both schizophrenics. Don't speak much but we cook for each other and sometimes he sings to me. He loves my daughter's children.'

'That's great Mandy but you need the police help to stay safe. Please call them now.'

'You don't care.'

'No! I am six thousand miles away and can do nothing from here.'

At about five the same morning, the South African Police call.

'Is that Jill? Come and get your brother.'

'I am in Australia and can't come. What do you usually do when people are violent?'

'Lock them up.'

'Well then, I guess you need to charge Peter and lock him up or get him committed.'

'Are you sure? He is mentally ill?'

'Yes I know and I am sure.'

LETTING GO

With my relationship sorted Dave and I are enjoying each other again. Our expectations of each other are that we take responsibility for our own feelings, talk about these and share our individual experiences. We also make time together to have fun.

We agree not to let our lives overwhelm us again and to care for ourselves when things get tough.

Shards of light

For my fiftieth birthday David gives me a shining red Peugeot cabriolet, which I call 'Swedie' and I invite Des and Mike to join us in celebrating my coming of age.

They arrive in Melbourne in time to enjoy the frenetic preparations for my momentous festivity. Des has never flown before or left the country and arrives bubbling with excitement. Everything is enchanting, our home nestled into the park, the muted blue heavens 'just as you described them' and the vibrant city a short tram ride away. She loves Richard's girlfriend, finds Lisa's exuberance wonderful and immediately gets into the spirit of planning for the murder mystery Lisa has adapted for my party.

On the evening in question we sit together in my study comparing hairstyles and costumes. Then Des looks around and says 'This room is so you Jill. Filled with light and colour it is so warm and inviting. I miss you so much . . . the excitement, never knowing what you'll be up to next, just giggling together, walking or singing and here we are as if no time has passed in the last twenty years.'

Dave knocks 'Come on ladies, time to go.' We doff headbands and saunter across to Barbara's magnificent old Edwardian. Lisa opens the stained glass door, escorts us down a long Persian carpeted hallway to the grand 'trompe-l'oeil' mustard ragged dining room where hosts of friends all in twenties costumes chatter effusively over Champagne filled glasses. With my entry the fun begins.

Lisa has carefully tailored the mystery to the eccentricity of this wonderful old house with its gracious high-ceilinged splendour, the mood of celebration and friends as characters in this the most intricate and over the top drama. We have a wonderful evening laughing, sleuthing and solving 'who done it'. When we reach the evenings climax and uncover the murderer everyone gasps. Our villain - the gentlest, most beguiling demure guest smiles widely and utters a malevolent chortle. Followed by raucous laughter, a magnificent birthday cake and a lusty happy birthday. What a wonderful evening.

Next day we rise early and head for the Tasmania ferry. We planned this holiday carefully with stays in beautiful old cottages. At Cradle Mountain we wander through muted Pencil pine forests. Take care picking our way through sodden root-bound tunnels of thick, corded trunks and grey bearded needle canopy and out to wonderful vistas of tannin darkened lakes sparkling in the gentle light of the autumn sun. Our senses sharpened by Mike's quiet pace and photographer's eye.

This leisurely trip is filled with laughter, reminiscence and wonder as we explore the breath taking beauty of the mighty Franklin River, visit Hobart's Salamanca market and wander through the picturesque Georgian cottages of Battery Point. Spend a day on the water before motoring to Port Arthur and on up the coast to Freycinet. As we toil up the slope we talk about Peter. 'We hiked together. Sometimes I really miss him.'

'How is he?'

'Doing well, even took himself and Mandy to the Kruger Park. He was excited at "bagging the infamous five." Said they happened upon a lion on the way to a waterhole. Got quite a fright.'

Des responds 'So pleased he's well.'

Our final stop is Launceston where we rest before returning to the mainland.

***

'OK Des here comes the 'piece de resistance'. We leave the boys to follow, don peak caps and sunglasses, climb into Swedie, wind windows and roof down, and speed off towards the sea. Abandoning all cares we giggle with glee, sing our lungs out into the whistling wind, arrival and saunter out onto the balcony to enjoy the view of the mighty Bass Straight. Des sighs 'I'll never forget this holiday. What a wonderful world you live in.'

When we wave Des and Mike goodbye at the airport I sigh 'This holiday was wonderful, I am so happy.'

Thesis and praxis

'Will you ever give studying away?'

'Why? Where else will I learn about myself or slay my demons'

'Chill, stop taking everything so seriously, and while you're at it, work doesn't always have to be hard either. Why always the most hopeless, hapless and helpless?'

'Well, when I fight for others, the demons that plague my sleep slip away. Perhaps this is my way of fighting the Boogieman.

***

I cannot escape the politics of the Howard government. Pauline Hanson is seducing Australians into fearing refugees. Those who come by sea are 'particularly dangerous'. They must be because we lock them up. I now know in my bones that I must turn again and tilt at windmills. I want to work to support these people.

Here, my issues confront me through others. I walk alongside those who face helplessness, struggle with mental illness, drown in isolation and cling to their God. I also revel with them in their resilience, hope and expectation that despite unspeakable hardship, the constant nagging rejection of racism, bureaucracy and xenophobia, they will build a sense of belonging, create a life of peace, and work towards prosperity. I also work with people concerned about Australia's abominable response to asylum seekers.

Within this work, I am drawn to people whose issues mirror my past experiences.

I visit Mary to find her crying in front of her house. As I approach, Ben her son comes up wielding an iron bar. 'I'm going to smash this house up.'

'OK, well I'll sit here with Mum. Hi Mary.'

I sit and take her hand. Ben smashes his bar against the fence. This has happened before and we both know the only way to settle Ben down is to keep calm. But this time Mary says 'He's been threatening me for ages and I'm scared.'

'How long?'

'Three hours.'

'Called for help?'

'The ambulance an hour ago but they haven't come.'

'I'll try again.'

First, I ask Ben 'Will you give me the bar?'

'No' I wait a while

'I am just going to make a call.' I call the police.

'How long? This young man is wielding an iron bar. We're concerned for our safety?'

'Soon.'

'Please we need your help, now!'

'Soon.'

Ben continues to rant and threaten. Mary and I sit quietly together. He smashes Mary's phone on the concrete driveway, comes close and threatens to smash us. We don't react and eventually he calms, comes, and sits next to his Mum. When he's been sitting for a while, I ask 'Can I put the bar somewhere safe?' Ben nods. I take it from him and put it in my car. Now the police arrive. They've been watching but weren't willing to come until Ben was settled.

'Please take Ben to Hospital, he has a psychiatrist there.'

'We'd prefer you take him. He trusts you.'

'You must be joking, on a freeway with a ranting young man? Put him in the divvy van where he'll be safe.'

'Only if his mum goes in the van with him and you promise to be there to get him out.'

'OK see you there.'

'Oh Peter, if only there'd been someone to do this for us.'

***

My involvement with asylum seekers has also awakened memories of wars, trauma and the callous way governments forget humanity.

The room has a mattress bed on the floor with two cushions and one old wooden chair. A couple of garments hang over the back. Along the wall opposite is a hot plate with one pot, sink with two cups a plate and knife, fork and two spoons, and in front of a high window is an old desk and on the desk a small TV set. Next to the desk is a door, which leads to a toilet and shower. These are the possessions gathered over several long years in Australia. Jamila is an asylum seeker who came to our rich country six years ago. She has been waiting for a resident's visa these long years. With the visa she can work and perhaps bring her three children to Australia, her only dream.

Today I am with Jamila again, but this time something is different. She wants to make sure that I understand completely and she says her English is not good enough to be sure that I hear right.

So I sit at one end of the hard mattress covered with sheets and an old cotton doona and she sits at the other end propped against the wall. Between us is an iphone. Through the speaker comes a disembodied voice of the interpreter, this time for me in English. A short answer to a long question, one I did not expect. 'I last saw my daughters six years ago.' I see tears dripping from Jamila's chin. Her eyes stare past me and I begin to brim with empathetic tears. I cannot think how to answer. I take a while and Jamila and the disembodied voice wait patiently. 'Sorry Jamila! I don't understand, but I am sorry.' The voice from the phone echoes 'I'm sorry too' and to Jamila in Farsi 'I'm sorry.'

'One day' says Jamila 'Inshallah.'

'Do you want to talk about it' followed by a quiet echo in Farsi.

'Perhaps next week.'

'So have I heard?'

'Yes you have heard, thank you.'

The interpreter cries, also says thanks and we switch off the iphone.

'Enough today, come next week please.'

'I will. Same time?' She nods. I say goodbye and go.

In the car I think about Jamila's desolate longing for her children and her inability to get work and hark back to my days in South Africa when people ached to be with their families but had no way of supporting them because of the pass laws.

***

Again I sit with Jamila on the old bed.

'Today you and me.' My heart sinks, does this mean that I will not learn more about her children. 'OK Jamila.'

'First, my friend. She has job in factory. I need job.' I want to interrupt. To say again that I do not do housing or jobs but she stops me. 'I know but you listen and I need to speak. It's hard with no Centrelink, no job, no visa and no house.' I look at the floor. What can I say? 'You listen is good.' I look into her beautiful face. This lady is so generous when I have nothing to offer. I ask again about Immigration, the housing people and the job search centre, who all say they'll help. She reaches out and touches my hand. 'I need you hear me.' I'm ashamed, why can't I just be there. The guilt consumes me. We sit together in silence and then she offers me tea. I shake my head but she rises and comes back with a cup for me and a glass for her. The tea is strong and sweet. 'Thank you.'

***

The next time I visit Jamila is waiting at the door. I enter and she immediately invites me to sit. 'Today I tell you. I run away from the rape and I not go home. I go to another place and then I ask my sister can I visit. She says yes. Now I can't go home. I not say goodbye to my children.' Jamila cries, loudly today as I sit and cry inside. Gulp down tears, helped by sweet tea.

And so we sit. I cannot leave or speak but I am with Jamila and she says 'Thanks God that you are here.'

Later she tells me her girls now nineteen and twelve and ten live with Jamila's mother who is ill. Sometimes they are hungry because famine comes to the city. 'Oh Jamila.'

'Thank you.'

'Again next week?'

214

'Yes please.'

Today Jamila wakes from a nightmare sleep and together we sit. There is no smile of recognition. I wait till she is fully awake then ask 'What is it Jamila?' She stares past me and says. 'No hope'

'Tell me please.'

'The immigration say not now. Wait. They no understand, no visa means no job, no Centrelink, no medical, just small food parcel, no life, no hope.'

'What happened?'

'Don't know.'

I cannot take this hopelessness, so look at the floor and say nothing for some time. Then 'I don't know what to say. I'm sorry. Can we talk to your God?' She stands, draws me to my feet, puts her hands in front of her eyes and begins to mutter and shake. I stand facing her and perhaps a foot apart and mutter also to my God. 'Why father why?' Then she puts her arms around me and weeps. I weep also. Then together we sit and she takes my hand. 'You ask immigration what I need to do.'

'I will.'

Later that day I ring and the answering voice is compassionate. 'I know, it's similar for many. With the boat people coming and cuts in our budget, unfortunately people wait longer. Jamila's papers are all there. She must wait for the minister.'

'But she cannot work and has no money to live.'

'I'll write a letter, so she can work.'

'Thanks, do you have any idea how long she will wait?'

'No.'

'Thanks, I can hear it's hard for you also. Goodbye'

'Goodbye. Phone again if you need to.' This bureaucrat finds it difficult to go. How difficult it would be to have many clients like Jamila. Perhaps she seldom gets a compassionate response herself.

***

There are many long, desolate sessions where Jamila fights her depression and waits for the visa that will not come. Then finally after many, many months she phones 'I am a permanent resident. Allahu Akbar. We have coffee together to celebrate and Jamila insists on paying.'

Jamila soon finds work, so I lose touch.

Two years after our coffee together my phone rings. 'Jill remember. Jamila. I got my visa? Today I phone to ask you to afternoon tea next week. Please come. Two of my daughters are here. I'm having a welcoming party.'

'Thank you Jamila' and then I can say no more. We both weep with happiness.

***

I feel deeply privileged to walk beside those brave enough to forsake all and start again. And sometime after excruciating pain and sorrow comes the exquisite sweetness of freedom hard fought for and won. When I do this work, I sleep well at night.

The last straw

Tired after a long flight I rush for passport control.

'Damn I'm not a blooming alien. Only five South Africans and six officers for that queue and here I stand.'

Then finally I'm at the red line waiting. 'Good morning! How are we today? See you have an emergency passport, how come?'

'Robbed in Spain!'

'Oh, I heard Spain is bad. Well you're here now, be careful.'

I avoid his gaze. DFAT said Spain was bad but South Africa was downright dangerous. The officer wishes me luck and I search for my companions. Next stop, an ATM. Unlikely we'll be robbed in the airport. Then out to a hire car with its global navigation system - SatNav - and we're off.

The countryside is bleak. Open fields beneath blue sky of my memory replaced by shanties and smog. We speed to our hotel on the far side of town, leave our companions and baggage. Rush back to an unknown suburb, search for a lost address, with my phone stolen. I remember Bedford View and Sunrise something to the east. We find the suburb and street and begin a gate-to-gate search, asking security guards for help. The Johannesburg of my recollection had doors one could knock at, but now high walls and electrified fences keep us out.

About to give up, Dave waves me over. Here is a man who thinks he knows Peter. He invites us beyond the electric fence and promises a neighbor who knows all. He is right. A woman welcomes us into her neat compact unit next to Peter's overgrown and messy facsimile and tells the tale of my brother's decline.

'Peter is a sad soul since Mandy's gone into an old age home. He's lonely, disheveled and doesn't care for himself. Been severely depressed for months.'

'Perhaps that's why he hasn't answered our calls.'

'Peter ranted and tried a left hook on a nurse at the home. He's off his meds, is threatening suicide. We called the police two days ago, he's at Gauteng Hospital'

We hurriedly thank her, take our leave, set the Sat Nav and are on way.

At first, we fly along the freeway but are then forced to slow as we turn off onto a small road between dilapidated houses. The air is thick with petrol fumes and dust as we enter one of the no-go areas we've sworn to avoid, lock the doors, grit our teeth and follow the map. The roads, now potholed are filled with only black faces. We have no idea where we are and I'm convinced we'll be car-jacked. The small clinic on the site marked by the Sat Nav isn't right, and no hospital in sight.

We've been warned not to leave our car, slow down or approach people in unfamiliar places to avoid robbery, but suddenly I see a group of people wearing the uniform of a long forgotten sect who laugh as they squeeze themselves into a small Toyota. 'Hello.' The Brethren of Zion are friendly as they point to the horizon.

'That way to hospital.'

We speed towards the gate, are stopped by a guard at a boom gate, the car including the boot is searched. He gives the all clear and announces that visiting hour is over!

'Thanks mate, we'll take our chances. We've come all the way from Australia to see my wife's brother', Dave says. The indifferent guard waves us on, we park beneath a 'Park at your own risk' sign and head indoors.

Throngs spill out of an exit, cheerful and chatting. Each looks us over. I tighten my grip on Dave's hand. It's not their black faces that frighten me. It's the high yellowing walls. The dilapidated feel. My brother's locked up in here?

Once inside, we follow the signs down one long musty corridor with peeling grey green walls and into another until finally, the Psych ward.

'I'm scared. Hope he's lucid. This creepy place reminds me of Sterkfontein when Peter was off the wall.' We enter the room and David asks a nurse for Peter. I stare ahead. My stomach turns at the smell. I'm back in my teens, urine trickling down my leg, mouth dry and heart racing as I stand before a raving man in a locked courtyard. I'm frozen with a fear so intense my heart will burst.

Terror rises, a putrid surge of bile in the back of my throat. I will it down and fight to breathe. Bugger off Boogieman. Leave me alone.

I grip David's hand and try to listen to the nurse. 'No Peter here, perhaps in the mental health outpost.'

'Please is there a toilet first.'

'No visitor's facility.'

'Please!'

She looks at my face,

'Follow me I'll take you to ours.'

I follow and wait as she unlocks the door, go in and gag. If this is the nurse's loo, what is the patient's like? I hold my nose, hover above the seat and let go.

'Down this passage and out the door. You'll find two houses across the car park. If you don't get help there go to Emergency. They have the computer. You'll find him that way for sure'

We cross the cold, windswept car park to two small unpainted asbestos grey prefabricated buildings signed 'Mental Health', skirt the buildings and knock at the doors and windows. No response. A security guard comes over and says 'They're shut, it's Saturday, come back Monday. It'll be open then.'

'My brother might be in there. I've come all the way from Australia.' He shrugs. 'Nobody there till Monday wherever you from.'

I start crying exhausted from the journey, horrified by the surrounds and suddenly desperate to see Peter. Dave takes my hand and half-drags me to the sacred computer in Emergency. Behind the smudged glass marked Reception sits a young man tapping at the keyboard. Dave pushes me forward.

'Please help me? My brother was admitted here on Friday but I can't find him.'

'What's his name?'

I give Peter's full name and spell it out.

'Address?'

The young man begins typing. It's clear his computer skills are poor. 'Spell his name again?' I write it down.

'No one by that name here.'

'But his neighbor told us they sent him here.'

'By who?'

'A doctor at outpatients . . .' I trail off, realizing how ridiculous I sound.

'No one of that name here!

'I . . . can I look.'

'Suit yourself.'

I go behind the counter and take a look.

'Anyone with a similar name, long Jewish names can be spelt in many ways. He looks at my stricken face and obliges. We try several different combinations of names and addresses. Nothing.

He goes into an office behind and comes back ten minutes later, 'Nothing there either!' He takes a few steps back and chats with another worker, 'Sorry nothing more I can do.'

'But . . . I have come all the way from Australia. Please!'

He sighs. 'Take a seat and I'll check the wards.'

I join David on an old wooden bench in front of the peeling grey green wall and we wait. I look around. A constant stream of wounded souls with blood-covered bodies is ushered through swing doors to treatment rooms. A man with a huge open gash above his right eye staggers in. Hit by an axe, perhaps.

The treated wander back through the same doors holding saline drips at arms length. One holds his bag at hip height as body fluids flow back into the bag. I retch. I thought Australian emergency departments were bad. I shiver and move closer to Dave. He squeezes my hand.

Finally, after about three quarters of an hour my helper returns. 'No sign of him! I have searched every ward. Come again Monday . . .'

'What's the point if he's not here. Where else?'

'Springs Hospital might not have triaged him yet. Maybe he's gone home.'

'Thanks.'

I swallow my tears and we leave. It's now dusk and the gloom accentuates my despair and failure. Having crossed the planet to see my baby brother, I can't even locate him. Dave is downcast, too, so we drive the forty kilometres back to the hotel in silence. Before the gate, David suggests he phone Peter's neighbour tomorrow to continue the search. I nod.

Next day Dave makes several enquiries but turns up nothing. Peter went to a clinic, was sent on to hospital, but disappeared en route.

'How does someone just disappear,' I wail. Dave agrees it's preposterous but what can we do?

Months ago we planned to join Dave's university mate in the mountains. Thirty-three year disappear. It's wonderful to watch old friends enjoying each other.

We're camped in the foothills of the magical Drakensburg Mountains. The magnificent Mont-Aux-Sources amphitheatre stretches a full hundred and eighty degree around us. As the sun sets the mountains are suffused in burned umber light, and peaks Dad and Mum climbed as first assents stand out like sentinels against the breathtaking craggy mountain wall. Every breath of air is filled with the musky smell of mountain grass and the whispering wind off the escarpment awakens childhood memories of the gentle mountain breezes we sang about around open campfires. Africa is my continent. I belong here. These recollections evoked by our glorious surroundings are tranquil, a complete contrast to the jangling disquiet of searching for my illusive brother. Peter was always peaceful in the mountains. Like a homing pigeon, he always knew exactly where he was in sunshine, mist or rain. His stride sure and his pleasure evident in every jaunty step he took.

In the quieter moments, my mind returns again to my lost brother. Where is he? What am I doing out of phone or Internet connection? Has he been found? Are they trying to ring me? What if he knows I'm here? 'We need to leave,' I beg Dave.' We must find Peter.'

As soon as we're back in range, I phone Peter's neighbor to find he has returned and left again. I talk things through with Dave and decide we need help from someone who knows South Africa's mental health system.

We are visiting Steven, Des's son on our way back to Johannesburg.

'Phone Mum she'll know someone I'm sure.'

I phone Des 'I need someone who knows the South Africa mental health system. A psychiatric guardian to manage Peter's affairs in South Africa is imperative.'

'Oh Jill there's always something I'm sorry . . . do you remember Freeman from church? He's a psychiatrist.'

'Yes . . . Is he still around . . . Can I trust him?'

'Totally but I think he is in the Cape; he left a while ago. I'll do some checking and get back.'

After a couple of calls, she is back, ' Jimmy is still in contact with him. I've got his number.'

'Fantastic I'll try him. See you tomorrow.'

I immediately try but his answering machine takes my details. I'll phone again from Des's home.

I try contacting Peter again. No answer. Phone his neighbor who says 'Told Peter you were here But he's out wondering the streets again.'

In Johannesburg I farewell David and our two friends who are flying home a week before me, walk down a corridor and into Des's arms. 'How's Peter, can we help?'

In Pretoria, I keep phoning Peter and leave messages on his answer phone and with the neighbor but he does not respond. He is still suicidal and needs hospitalization.

Freeman calls back and remembers me, 'Happy to advise you, agree Peter needs psychiatric and financial guardian. The Jewish Woman's Benevolent Society may help.'

I try them but they don't answer.

***

Thoughts full of Peter, I still catch up with friends and political compatriots. These meetings are exciting but with each interaction, I see more of South Africa's dysfunction, corruption and inequality. A break-in to friend's car directly outside Des's house, continual electricity outages and the landline dead for days, lays bare the decaying infrastructure and poor management of essential services. Sad! The politicians now take the money and the populace suffers because of poor administration, lack of care and greed. Many stories are heartbreaking.

After the initial euphoria at a multi-cultural government led by Mandela, the father of the New South Africa, all is not well. AIDS is a rampant, corruption the catch cry and waves of violence are spread across the country. People are disillusioned by the slow pace of change.

In August 2012 police open fire on workers at a platinum mine in Marikana, killing at least 34 people, leaving at least 78 injured and arresting more than 200 others. Prosecutors drop murder charges in September against 270 miners after a public outcry, and the government sets up a judicial commission of inquiry in October.

Familiar! The people are now workers not Blacks but the sentiment is similar.

***

Each day, I try to leave a message with the Jewish Women's Benevolent Society (JWBS). When no answer comes, I fight feeling completely helpless. Finally, I get through, 'I'll pass your information on to the social worker.'

I keep trying Peter. No answer and if he's not there, there's no point going over.

Finally the JWBS social worker phones. 'Any service to Peter is confidential.' I smile. How often I have used these words myself? Next day she phones and says 'Without formal proof that either Else or Peter are Jews, we can't help. A Jewish birth certificate, a bris, or bar mitzvah certificate for Peter or a Jewish death certificate for Elsa or her mother. I am not sure any such thing exists but will start digging when I get back to Australia.

Wow! How do I prove we are Jews?

As I leave, I reflect on how good it has been to stay in Pretoria. Amazing to walk into Des and Mike's family and feel so completely held and understood. Their care and concern for Peter is overwhelming.

I love the gentle rhythm of each day. The breakfast begun with a quiet 'Thank you Lord', a simple generous meal of fruit, cereal and a cup of tea or coffee, some toast and a discussion about what activities await. The whole of each day progresses with God at centre. I wish that I could live thus.

Despite this, my week is frantic and my dream of the New South Africa shattered by the breakdown of trust between a voracious government and disempowered citizens who cannot rely on even the most basic administration of the country's resources.

Most harrowing is the constant nagging doubt that I will find any solution to Peter's pressing problems.

Peter

I am back home and in a sweat of anxiety.

Do my emotions echo other siblings of people with severe psychiatric illness? Do they feel responsible, lie awake wondering what might have been if treatments were better? This brings no reprieve. Let me face the issue at hand.

What do I do about Peter?

We spend weeks trying to prove Peter, Else, and Ouma are Jews but find no papers to prove religious heritage. Mum never went to synagogue after leaving Germany and was not buried a Jew. Peter never had a bris or a bar mitzvah.

How can I find the money to keep Peter safe? Dave and I come up with a plan and I contact the hospital and talk with the social worker. She will get a letter from the psychiatrist and we will approach the German government. Dad had a German pension and Peter was always his dependant.

It is a relief not getting the Peter's exhausting calls but memories of his cries for help and my guilt at not saving Peter are excruciating. Unbearable remembering we were close or the ravages of schizophrenia, bipolar, the straight jacket of treatments that stole his soul.

Distressing are the oppressive, unrelenting reminders that greed, corruption and simple mismanagement of South Africa's economy has stolen Peter's life line. His trust fund is no longer adequate and I who cannot save him am fraught and a fraud.

I cannot breathe. Despair overwhelms me. I am without hope. Sorry Peter I must let go. I go to bed and pull the covers over my head. Finally, despite overwhelming terror, I force myself to breathe, count slowly to ten and still my pounding heart. I turn to the Boogieman bid him come closer and look him directly in the face. 'I will no longer freeze in fear. Bugger off and let me be!' I weep until I am spent.

What's new

Banishing the Boogieman didn't work overnight. When I felt the familiar 'responsibility for Peter' or lack of trust in myself, I would check my responses with David. When the Boogieman threatened, I would go to my computer and write about Peter or me or about trauma.

'Oh hell! Nothing's changed. Where in your body is it? Stomach, chest, head and my response fight, flight or freeze? OK what am I afraid of? Now write.'

I would write until tired enough to sleep or what had triggered me had faded. Go back to bed and tell the Boogieman that because I understood he couldn't get me.

When awake, I spoke with others about trauma and its impact.

After some months, I felt more in control.

***

One day I wake from a different dream.

I stand in a vast plain stretching out in all directions. The cool dawn sky is a muted blue scattered with see-through clouds, the ground dusky sand with occasional tufts of grey green grasses. The wind redolent with rain whispers softly against my skin. I am peaceful and alive with expectation.

No clutter and clash of past dreams where I seek dark places to hide my secret shame. This heralds a change, a gentler engagement with my world, focus wholeheartedly onto present.

On Skype, I revel in my grandson Max. Watch him savor the sounds of words in Chinese and English. Go weak at the knees at his deep belly laugh. Richard's pride at his son delights me.

Then Max and his parents come to Australia to visit; his direct, forceful, all-consuming vigor overwhelms me. He experiences life through all his senses. He chuckles, gabbles and howls. He laughs at my English and tries to explain that my words are wrong. After a day or two of teaching me Chinese, he begins to talk some English. He tastes everything, demands music and is delighted by Mozart. He sings 'twinkle, twinkle' with the Wiggles and loves us joining in. He acts out stories, stops in the park to pick me a flower and demands 'carry me' as I the aging grandma gulp with exhaustion and smile as he sings to the world about the wind. 'Cold, fun: cold, fun!'

We are naughty together. I water the garden and he asks for the hose then turns it on me. For a moment the anger rises but then I look at his cherub face, take the hose hold it in the air and together we cavort in its gentle rain. When we come inside after singing in the rain we are both chastised, 'Naughty Nai Nai, naughty Max.' We giggle, dry ourselves, and change.

On another occasion we both sit on the stairs, I move down a step to tie Max's shoe, and before I know it, we are playing another game. 'Bump, bump, bump.' We both giggle, as we bump down the stairs on our backsides and then rush to the top and start again. I love these childish pranks and wait expectantly for the next opportunity to simply have fun.

My beloved daughter Lisa marries and I extend my Asian connection to include Pakistan. In a wonderful Islamic ceremony in our family room, my lovely Lisa marries a vital young man from Lahore. Lisa wears a beautiful vibrant full length African dress, mauve and dove grey enameled necklace made by Mum many years before and a muted turquoise headscarf. Adnan's family joins us on Skype as vows are exchanged. Two months later, I am thrilled to hear another grandchild is on the way.

David and I plan for retirement.

Peter is still in a psychiatric hospital and I am in contact with his social worker. Together we work towards finding him stable accommodation in the community when he is well. I feel free of guilt or shame. Content to do what I can and leave the rest to God.

I no longer fear going mad or feel the imperative to save others. I rest for a while and enjoy what life has to offer.

Halleluiah.

Finale

Today Peter's social worker emails me from South Africa. Peter is in Pretoria hospital. I phone and am put through to intensive care. A doctor answers. 'Your brother is in a coma. He fell from the ceiling and broke his ribcage. He cannot breathe so a machine breathes for him. His kidneys have collapsed. He is unlikely to recover.'

I don't connect with the words. Don't understand what is said but know that I'm alone. Not an orphan but perhaps tomorrow or tomorrow's, tomorrow my last connection with the past will be gone forever. I will be totally adrift.

I phone ritually each day, and slowly Peter begins to breathe without the machine. He gets oxygen through a tracheotomy, comes out of the coma and begins to move his feet and hands. His eyes open but he does not follow or respond to people's touch. Despite this, the nurses say he is getting a little better day-by-day. He is moved to critical care.

Each time I ask they say 'Do not come. He won't know you. Wait a while.'

Lindy visits and confirms this. I keep my distant vigil, relieved that I am spared the vision of Peter's tragedy.

At the beginning of the sixth week Peter is well enough to be moved again, only this time, despite his improvement, he doesn't survive.

Today on the 14 September 2013, Yom Kippur, the Day of Atonement I phone again and am told that Peter died an hour ago.

My brother is dead. Finally! He has his wish. His suicide was successful. 'Goodbye my brother, rest in peace. Perhaps now I can truly let you go.'

***

A month later, I arrive in Johannesburg and Des is waiting for me arms open in welcome.

In Pretoria, I chill and listen to all the local gossip. Something is different on this visit. After eighteen months people are more hopeful. Zuma's government is still corrupt but there is a lady,

Helen Zille working hard to hold them to account. Perhaps justice will soon prevail.

We go to collect Peter's ashes, smiling as we play with the notion that Peter is finally contained. The lady funeral director is taken aback by our levity. We return home with a mini casket. It will fit nicely into Mike's garage cupboard until we scatter the ashes.

David arrives on Friday, on Saturday we have a small wake for Peter. After Dad's farewell I am prescriptive about what is said.

'Peter had a troubled life and difficult death. Today I wish to share a few anecdotes that I look back on with joy.

I loved Peter's voice. When the family sang together I loved the generous harmony we so easily created together.

Peter had many fantasies:

'When my airplane comes true' . . . and he would draw word pictures of wonderful escape stories for him and for me. We would fly to Europe, America or Mars protected by mighty defenses. Guns, missiles, radar detectors and smoke screens would hide us and keep us safe.

We would hug each other close; I would stroke his hair and my little brother Peter would talk in his big person voice. These stories would fade into sleep as we clung together. I would know he loved me, my big, brave, baby brother.'

After me, others added a few gentle words and Mike closed with prayer.

With this small sendoff behind us, Mike, Des, David and I drove up to the farm where we were to spread Peter's ashes. Unable to pry his small casket open David dug a hole at the foot of a soaring Sequoia planted by my father forty years before.

'Rest easy Peter. I know you always loved the farm so close to the wild cloud mountain.'

REFLECTIONS

Looking back I realize that many things have changed for me in the past two years. I have let go of my need to understand what happened to Peter. Many factors contributed to Peter's illness, some were genetic, and some environmental. The brother, engaged and responsive to the outside world, disappeared long ago. Peter is dead. He is beyond reach. Before he died I already grieved his loss.

The treatment of psychiatric illness has progressed. Now new drugs make a huge difference in the lives of many people with a mental illness. This cannot change what happened to our Peter, but it's wonderful to know that new treatments allow other sufferers to live more satisfying lives.

In writing this book while I am working with refugees torn by the trauma of war, I have gained a deeper understanding. Often it is children who struggle most to shake off their trauma. Their parents are consumed with the demands of survival, and the effort to establish a new life.

I have observed many holocausts that plague our world. I believe we have to help victims to articulate, remember, and work towards forgiveness and reparation of violence. Politics is intensely personal.

AFTERWORD – THE PATH OF PETER'S ILLNESS

I wrote this book in search of self; beginning with Peter, my younger brother, because his mental illness became a centrifugal force. He was born in 1951 in Johannesburg, South Africa.

Diagnosed with depression at ten, by eleven he was hospitalised, displaying clear symptoms of both bi-polar disorder and schizophrenia, with uncontrolled mood swings. After six weeks of medication and electric shock treatment (ECT) he was discharged – disoriented, but compliant and stable.

His second admission in August 1962 was brief. Peter's mood was elevated but soon he was 'chemically contained.' He was released into our family's care.

In 1964 he was re-admitted with psychotic symptoms – hallucinations, (hearing voices). E.C.T. and new medications eventually controlled these. He was released again, with weekly supervision as an outpatient.

There were many more hospitalisations, the most significant in 1967. Peter became a public nuisance. He approached shoppers at the local shops, becoming threatening when they refused to purchase his handmade kites. He was forcibly sedated and committed to a closed ward for observation.

After treatment with high doses of a different antipsychotic, Peter's continued disruption affected the neighbourhood and our home life. He slept four hours or less at night, was restless when awake, playing his guitar or arguing loudly with his voices.

In hospital, he escaped. A good climber, he scaled walls the staff thought impregnable and waved to passers-by from the roof. After performing his favorite tune, he climbed down the other side of the building and out, arriving home disheveled and hungry.

Two months after his escape, the prognosis remained poor. Full of Largactil and having received countless jolts of electric current, Peter's symptoms were unchanged. My parents were distraught.

When we thought Peter could not get worse, he became catatonic. In the ward he lay still; his eyes unseeing; his features fixed. If I spoke, shouted, poked or pushed his arm, there was no response.

When staff turned him to prevent bedsores, his limbs stayed in the same rigid position. This was terrifying, and he remained that way for weeks. At their wits' end, the doctors recommended Peter for Insulin Shock Therapy (IST).

"It's experimental, but early indicators are promising. Proven treatments haven't worked."

My parents consented, and Peter was injected with large doses of insulin, putting him into a coma for six days per week for eight weeks.

This worked, sort of. Peter slowly began to move, and be more communicative. He began sitting up in bed, mumbling disconnected sentences. But he showed no emotion or expression.

Three weeks after the course was completed, Peter was sent home. The hope was that a changed environment might revive Peter's character, minus the unwanted symptoms.

But the Peter we had known never returned. He struggled to motivate himself and re-learn what he'd lost through shock treatment; and to shake off (what I observed as) a waking catatonia.

Like an automaton, he moved mindlessly, changing direction only when he bumped into something. Despite this, the doctors were pleased. They'd stabilised his medication, and his outpatient visits dropped back to twice a year.

The Doctors' problems were ending but my family's were just beginning. After IST Peter never regained normal functioning. As time passed our family had to come to terms with the possibility that he never would.

Up to that point we had drawn strength from the hope that one day Peter would be well. This helped us face the daily ups and downs of his illness, treatment, recoveries and relapses. We hoped that one day he would have a somewhat normal life. The turmoil and distress his illness had caused us would end, enabling us to focus on ourselves and one another. We might find a way to comfort each other - to be a happy family at long last.

But as the chronic nature of Peter's illness, and the damage caused by its medical management, dawned on us we were forced to come to terms with the problem: Peter would never be well again. I was locked into a relationship where I felt helpless, guilty and unable to be free to pursue my future.

Peter wasn't the only problem my family never solved. Indeed, the stubbornness of his illness was both a reflection and a symbol of the Holocaust, and the grief of its wounds - that wouldn't heal.

An extravagant claim perhaps, but I work as a counselling psychologist with people who have survived trauma even now, forty years after Peter's lapse into chronic illness.

This book has examined how Nazism blighted my parents' opportunities and how the Holocaust impacted my family. Was Peter's illness inevitable? Was it the result of my parents' dislocation and losses, as European Jews? Was there anything that I did – as a child or young adult – that contributed to my younger brother's acute illness or impeded his quest for health? What could I take from our experiences to give me insight into trauma? To help me to confront my childhood trauma? To heal the terrible sadness at the loss of my brother's potential, both as a family member and as part of the community?

Finally, was 'The Boogieman' a manifestation of trauma; Peter's illness; racism or was it a suppressed memory of something that happened to me?

ACKNOWLEDGEMENTS

Special thanks to Leslie Cannold for mentorship and to Sharon, Barbara, David and Carrolynne for editing.

Robert Hillman I thank for his generous criticism and my ever-patient family and friends for their support and for listening to my endless ravings.

www.ingramcontent.com/pod-product-compliance
Lightning Source LLC
Chambersburg PA
CBHW051717020426
42333CB00014B/1024